Premchand on National Language
Rashtrabhasha

(Translated from Hindi into English)

Editors
Anuradha Ghosh
Saroj Kumar Mahananda
Trisha Lalchandani

AAKAR

Premchand on National Language: *Rashtrabhasha*

Edited by: Anuradha Ghosh, Saroj Kumar Mahananda, Trisha Lalchandani

First Published 2019

ISBN 978-93-5002-606-9

Published by
AAKAR BOOKS
28 E Pocket IV, Mayur Vihar Phase I
Delhi 110 091 India
aakarbooks@gmail.com

Laser Typeset at
Arpit Printographers, Delhi

Printed at
Sapra Brothers, Noida

Contents

Translators

Anuradha Ghosh, Associate Professor, Department of English, Jamia Millia Islamia

Mehak Sawhney, PhD Scholar, Department of Linguistics, University of Delhi

Rakesh Sengupta, PhD Scholar, School of Languages, Cultures, and Linguistics (South Asia), SOAS, London

Sango Bidani, MPhil Scholar, Department of English, Jamia Millia Islamia

Sarah Mariam, PhD Scholar, Department of English, Jamia Millia Islamia

Saroj Kumar Mahananda, Assistant Professor, Department of English, Jamia Millia Islamia

Sohebur Rehman Niazi, PhD Scholar, Freie University, Berlin

Suvankur Sukul, PhD Scholar, Department of South Asian Languages and Civilisations, University of Chicago

Trisha Lalchandani, Project Fellow, UGC SAP-DRS Phase 3, Department of English, Jamia Millia Islamia

Acknowledgements

We wish to acknowledge the role of UGC SAP-DRS III, Department of English, Jamia Millia Islamia, New Delhi in providing the required support towards the publication of Premchand's views on Hindi as the national language.

The two international workshops organised on 10-11 March 2017 and 15-16 March 2018 helped us in finalising the translations and we wish to thank Dr. Harjeet Singh Gill, Professor Emeritus, Centre for Linguistics and English, Jawaharlal Nehru University, Dr. Afroz Taj and John Caldwell, Department of Asian Studies, University of North Carolina, Dr. Mehr Afshan Farooqi, Asia Institute, University of Virginia, Dr. Rajesh Sharma, Panjabi University, Patiala, who were Visiting Fellows to the UGC SAP-DRS III, Department of English, JMI and resource persons in the two workshops mentioned above.

We owe special thanks to our colleagues Dr. M. Asaduddin, Dr. Ameena K. Ansari, Dr. Nishat Zaidi and Dr. Baran Farooqi, Department of English, Jamia Millia Islamia who are practising translation scholars with multilingual competence. Their role as mentors, both within and outside workshops, their support, motivation and affection has helped the three of us greatly to put together this volume.

Our obligation to Shri O.R. Niazi, former Director of Programmes, All India Radio, and Visiting Fellow to the UGC SAP-DRS III, Department of English, JMI needs a special mention. He mentored our work in the final stage during

April-May 2018 and helped us overcome our obstacle of not knowing Urdu.

We acknowledge the assistance provided by the Premchand Archives and Literary Centre, Jamia Millia Islamia.

A special thank you to our students—PhD scholar Mahmoud Al-Zayed and postgraduate scholar Monib Ahmad–as without their help we could not have completed our work.

Introduction

ON TRANSLATING PREMCHAND'S 'RASHTRABHASHA'

In lieu of an 'Introduction' to our experiences of translating Premchand's writings on the question of having Hindi as the national language in the twenty-first century, it is important to share some of our thoughts as translators and editors. It was not an easy task to contend with the spectre of Premchand, one of the foremost intellectuals of the twentieth century, for a little over two years and that too, engage with his opinions on a contentious subject like the proposal of 'Hindustani'[1] as the national language of India. What we wish to share through this 'Introduction' is the series of challenges we have come across in ascertaining the texts that do justice to a volume that intends to put together Premchand's views on the need for a national language in opposition to English as an anti-colonial strategy that was in sync with the subcontinent's diverse rhythms of resistance against British rule.

(I) EDITORS' PARADOX: SELECTION OF SOURCE TEXTS

The editors' paradox in relation to Premchand's views on topical issues of his times arises with the selection of source

1. "[A] cover term used by Mahatma Gandhi to resolve the rivalry between Hindi and Urdu" (p. 306). See Hans R. Dua, "The National Language and the Ex-Colonial Language as Rivals: The Case of India", *International Political Science Review* (1993), Vol. 14, No. 3, 293-308. (https://about.jstor.org/terms)

texts that were to be considered for translation. On the question of the national language, Premchand has written in Hindi Hindustani and they were later transliterated into Urdu and whatever published versions are available were consulted and compared. Premchand's bilingualism and his intense engagement with both the languages is noteworthy and as we closely read the different published versions in Hindi and cross-checked it with Urdu to identify if there were any variations, we realised that it was a complicated exercise. In fact the complication of it all made us re-think the times in which Premchand wrote and the kind of politics he espoused when he campaigned along with his colleagues, for Hindustani and not necessarily Hindi as the unquestionable choice as a national language for India as it configured in 1947.

Our first take-off point was Dr. Ram Vilas Gupt's compilation of Premchand's non-fiction writings in *Premchand ke Vichaar* in three volumes, published by Prakashan Sangathan in 2003. Alongside this, we consulted Shri Ramvilas Sharma edited *Premchand Rachnavali* Volumes 7, 8 and 9, published in New Delhi by Janvani Prakashan and reprinted in 2006, as his non-fiction writings on the question of national language and literature, written between 1931 and 1936 appear here. We compared the Hindi versions with the Urdu from *Kulliyat-e-Premchand*, edited by Shri Madan Gopal and published by the National Council for Promotion of Urdu Language (NCPUL), New Delhi in 2003 in order to ensure whether there were any pieces that were written solely in Urdu, and have not been rendered into Hindi. While Gupt's edition attempts to categorise Premchand's opinions and views about national and international issues, challenges posed by caste, gender, religion and language that threaten to fracture all possibilities for a united subcontinental wave of resistance against the British, the obituaries he wrote in memory of people as a meaningful self-explanatory form of facilitating readers navigating through the wide and diverse terrain of Premchand's thoughts as expressed in non-fiction, Sharma's edition takes a chronological trajectory and in Volumes 7, 8 and 9, Premchand's non-fiction writings, speeches, memoirs, editorials, introductions and critical assessments appear.

The section titled *Rashtrabhasha* in Gupt's edition is one of the most comprehensive collections of his writings on the subject among several others that were published. If *vichaar* translates as "perspectives" or "opinions" or "views," then the section that appears as *Rashtrabhasha* (national language) in the second volume of the series mentioned, was written between December 1932 to April 1936. The three-volume series is interesting as it includes Premchand's views on several issues of local, regional, national and international significance. Though the contents in the three volumes might appear as a series of uneven prose pieces that take myriad forms and follow different genres and styles of writing, they are all of equal significance as they reflect the position Premchand had taken in the debates and discussions of his times.

The section titled *Rashtrabhasha* is of special interest today as though Hindi in the Devanagari script was accorded the status of official language, and not national language, alongside English by *The Constitution of India,* it remained a matter of contention, as till date the attempt to standardise Hindi is enmeshed in several challenges. If as editors to this volume we had been guided by the book plan of Shri Gupt and not taken into consideration Ram Vilas Sharma's version, we would have been misled as the journey of Hindustani (which is an amalgamation of Hindi and Urdu in the spoken form) to Hindi Hindustani and finally Hindi as "Rashtrabhasha" would seem to be a linear one. It is through pieces on the question of national language as it is integrally tied to the issue of national literature, which again is an amalgamation of strains in different regional language literatures as well as oral literature in dialects and sub-languages of Hindi that makes one traverse through a terrain of thought that the architects of this nation, be it Mahatma Gandhi, Rajendra Prasad, Jawaharlal Nehru, Munshi Premchand, had been forced to contend with owing to the parting of ways between Hindi and Urdu leading to the confusion as to whether the binaries are between "Rashtrabhasha *versus* Qaumi Zabaan" in terms of an opposition or "Rashtrabhasha *and* Qaumi Zabaan," in terms of a coupling that unmistakably promotes Hindustani, a hybrid form in Devanagari script and not Persian, as the national language of Bharatvarsha (Indian subcontinent).

(II) TRANSLATOR'S PARADOX

Though one would entirely agree with what Shri Avadhesh Kumar Singh in "Premchand on/in Translation" very appropriately observes that "[U]n/translatability is a translator's problem, not of the translation. Untranslatability is a myth," (p. 129) one would like to engage with the question in terms of history, text and context—as all three are integrally interlinked in any process of translation. As translators within the Indian location one is caught in a double-bind as there is the question of fidelity to the source text and fidelity to the history of discourses that were in circulation during the period of February 1931 to June 1936 when the issue of having one national language, one script and a national literature were deliberated upon in journals like *Hans, Jagaran* and *Triveni.* The activities of the Hindi Prachar Sabha, Nagari Pracharini Sabha, Hindi Sahitya Sammelan Prayag and the Rashtriya Sahitya Parishad were crucial in translating the national vision behind the idea of a nation. The emphasis on the dialectics between the region and the nation as co-determinants and the fact that Hindi/Hindustani and not English, could be a 'common language,' but not necessarily a 'national language' or it could be a 'national language' as it was already a 'common language' is an interesting one. While translating the pieces, though individual translators had their own visions, an attempt was made to keep to the nuances of the source language culture as much as possible in order to convey what the word 'national' then implied in terms of a political imaginaire. Words like 'Hind,' 'Hindustan,' 'Bharat' and 'Bharatvarsh' have not been translated as 'India' as the political map of this sub-continent was not what it is today. Likewise, terms like 'Shriukt,' 'Shri,' 'Shrimati,' 'Mantri Ji,' 'Maulana,' 'Maulvi' and the suffix 'Ji' after names of people as a mark of respect have been retained to convey cultural nuances and ways of address that are common in this subcontinent. In-text translations have been provided for words like 'daflis,' 'tablas,' 'kos,' 'crore,' and other common nouns wherever necessary and there was an attempt to draw in the interesting idioms and phrases to demonstrate in English the resonances of Hindi Hindustani, Urdu and Hindi wherever feasible without surrendering the readability of the text in the target language. Though the act of translation is not "mere synonym hunting," as Gayatri Chakravorty Spivak mentioned in a public lecture titled "What is It to Translate?" delivered on 21 February 2018 in the M.A. Ansari Auditorium at Jamia Millia Islamia, it was important for us to be able to do justice to the spirit of the debates within the public domain as documented by Premchand in the form of minutes of meetings attended, reports of conferences, editorials and allied writings as well as the history of the times. The attempt of editors to present Premchand as an advocate of Hindi and not of Urdu, or to select those particular sections of his writings that are part of the campaigns for Hindi being conducted all over India, particularly in the south, or to suggest that his concerns of a 'pure' Hindi, unsullied by the verbal nuances that were colouring its spoken form in the non-Hindi-speaking belt is indicative of his privileging of Hindi as "Rashtrabhasha" and not Hindustani is only part of what could be a comprehensive account of Premchand. If the business of translation is not a mechanical one, then the very act of rendering Premchand's "vichaar" in English must follow his politics of nation-building which considered Hindustani to be the spoken language of the majority in a gesture of creating composite cultural and linguistic equivalences reflecting an integrative, rather than divisive nationalism which could work towards bridging the increasing gap between the Hindus and Muslims.

(III) HISTORICAL PARADOX

According to the writings on national language between 1931 to 1936, the challenges before the progressive social forces of this subcontinent were varied and diverse. To address the terms of reference dealing with language policy/ies in India, one needs to engage with the history of the subcontinent that has been variously documented as well as understood by those within and outside the diverse movements for freedom that this subcontinent has been home to. If one takes the period of rule of the East India Company and then the British Raj, as the period of 'proto-colonial'[2] and then colonial rule[3], and engages

---

2. The term 'proto-colonial' is a coinage which may have academic resonances in the field of African Studies and allied Area Studies disciplines, travel literature and 'The Crusades' to refer to the period of the East India Company's role in the Indian subcontinent and South Asia, primarily for reasons of trade during 1612-1757, and after the Battle of Plassey, the period is referred to as "Company Rule in India" during 1757-1858, when the British imperialist intentions were becoming clear. In fact, if one goes by literature on the period between "1857-'58" which has been variously referred to as the first war for Indian independence, "Indian Mutiny" or/and "Sepoy Mutiny", it becomes evident that the issue of nomenclature of categories describing an event is politically motivated and one has to be wary of history as colonial constructions, indigenous constructions, nationalist constructions, and ad infinitum, without losing focus on the fact that though *What is History*? (book by E. H. Carr) is debatable, there is a loose understanding of the discipline of history *to be what it is not*—and that is, *not* literature, *not* cultural studies, *not* travel and tourism, and so on and so forth on the one hand, and on the other, all of it together with shared trajectories and spaces, but with filiation to none/some/all—again depending on the perspective through which one wishes to engage with the object of one's inquiry.
3. The period of the British Raj is between 1858 to 1947, when the Indian subcontinent came under the direct rule of the British Crown when the 'Government of India Act' (short title) or 'An

with the issue of how language becomes "an important tool of imperialism" (p. 91)—both linguistic and social, then Tariq Rahman's essay 'British Language Policies and Imperialism in India' becomes an important point of departure. In this essay, Rahman examines British language policies in India during the eighteenth and nineteenth centuries taking the Orientalists and Anglicists controversy between 1780 and 1835 to argue that "[b]oth parties aimed at consolidating... British rule over India, but their opinions differed as to whether the vernacular languages and the vehicular languages used under Muslim rule on the one side, or English on the other side, were the best means to attain the goal" (p. 91). While Rahman's preoccupation was to study the shifts in policy based on Persian, Hindustani and Sanskrit in the 1780s to an intermediate phase of using local languages to the use of English from 1830 onwards taking the Orientalist-Anglicist controversy as the point of departure, he concludes that such a study "is useful for understanding the relationship between language policies and political power" and how it demonstrates that "conflicting linguistic policies... have the same political aim—that of consolidating the newfound empire" (p. 111). His comments on Pakistani historiography that considers the abolition of Persian to be "a British conspiracy to harm Muslims" (p. 109) is interesting. C. Treveylan's letter of 9 April 1834 to Lord William Bentinck

---

Act for the Better Government of India' (long title) was passed on 2 August 1858 to ensure a better governance of the region. Queen Victoria's proclamation to the Indian people which is still preserved in the Victoria Memorial, Kolkata, is an interesting artefact of the colonial times. The aforementioned Act, which was an Act of the Parliament of the United Kingdom (21 and 22 Vict. c. 106) was proposed in Parliament led by Prime Minister Lord Palmerston (20 October 1784–18 October 1865) first as 'An Act for the Better Government of India' and later introduced as another bill by Edward Henry Stanley, 15th Earl of Derby, (21 July 1826–21 April 1893) which was given Royal Assent on 2 August 1858 where the functions of the East India Company were transferred to the British Crown.

advocating the abolition of Persian and its replacement with English to be "the crowning stroke" (qtd. Rahman, p. 108) proved true and the after-effects of it all seems to have fomented further controversies over the issue of adopting Hindustani/ Hindi in both/either Devanagari and/or Persian script as it was the language of the majority as a national language for it was already in circulation as a common language, in place of English or any other established provincial language in the next hundred odd years.

In fact all this had a direct impact on the ways in which the issue of 'common' language vis-a-vis 'national' language was taking shape during 1931 to 1936 in the discourses on having a balanced language policy that is avowedly anti-colonial. The underlying strain of conflict over the issue of Hindi versus Urdu on the one hand, Hindi versus other established regional languages and Hindi versus English create a triad that marks the debates on the question of national language and it is hardly surprising that in the context after independence, Hindi in Devanagari script gets the status of "official" language alongside English, and not that of "national" language as it was conceived of in a bid to establish national identity as per the thrust of the waves of resistance movements for freedom that were waged for almost half a century prior to 1947. The need to replace English with Hindi as the official language was fraught with controversy as though there was unanimity over the need for a common language, there was no general consensus over the adoption of Hindi as the national language despite the attempt of linking it to the national struggle for independence and questions of national identity. Hans R. Dua's 'The National Language and the Ex-Colonial Language as Rivals: The Case of India' draws attention to the complex socio-linguistic backdrop that made the choice of one national language, its acceptance, promotion and development a contentious issue. According to Dua,

> While a common national language as a symbol of national identity was an integral component in the national struggle

> of colonial countries, the emphasis on the national language differed partly because of the different sociolinguistic situations and partly because of the ideological commitment of the political parties. The case of Hindi may be considered as a prototype of the complex sociolinguistic issues involved in national identity. (p. 293)

Though Dua charts the history of divergences between Hindi and Urdu through the recognition and status the former gained as an "equal official language with Urdu" (p. 294) in 1900 in the then United Provinces[4], Bihar and Central Provinces[5] by the British as a result of the movement for Hindi launched by Madan Mohan Malaviya, Bhartendu Harish Chandra and others, development of separate language associations for Hindi and Urdu, like, Nagari Pracharini Sabha founded in 1893 to promote the idea of one script, Hindi Sahitya Sammelan in 1910, Dakshin Bharat Hindi Prachar Sabha in 1918, Rashtra Bhasha Prachar Samiti in 1936 to promote the cause of Hindi along with the role that "religious leaders, reformers, literary personalities and linguists" like Maharishi Daya Nand Saraswati from Gujarat, Navin Chandra Roy, Bankim Chandra Chatterji, Keshav Chandra from Bengal had to play, he simply ignores the debates that proponents of Urdu might have made as well. It is in fact to bridge the widening gap between the Hindus and Muslims which is expressed through the linguistic rivalries between Hindi and Urdu following the political tenor of the activities of the Akhil Bharatiya Hindu Mahasabha founded in 1915 and All-India Muslim League in 1906 that Mahatma Gandhi was propelled into action[6] to advocate the cause of Hindustani, which was

4. Now Uttar Pradesh.
5. Now Madhya Pradesh.
6. See, the following post by Yogendra Yadav on 28 July 2012, 'Thaughats (sic.) of Mahatma Gandhi on National Language':

   "I am right in my preference for Hindustani. I do believe that as between the Nagari script and the Urdu script, the former will win. In the same way if we leave out the question

conceived of as an amalgamation of Hindi and Urdu. While in 1925, the proceedings of the amendments to the constitution of the Indian National Congress was recorded in Hindustani at the behest of Mahatma Gandhi, in 1937, when Congress ministries were formed in most provinces, it was "Hindi-Hindustani" that was advocated as the common lingua franca of the region.

Keeping this historical backdrop in mind, while locating Premchand's views on the question of Hindi, language of the people of Hind, and thereby Hindustani in its spoken form with two written scripts—Nagari and Persian, as the national language, one must keep in mind that for the architects of this nation, it was clear that there ought to be no tussle between either 'rashtrabhasha' or 'qaumi zabaan,' as after-all, no matter how we wish to call it, the need for one language and preferably one script replacing English was undoubtedly the need of the hour. After all, "What is the test of national

---

of the script and consider the language only, Hindustani will certainly win. That is so because Sanskritized Hindi is wholly artificial while Hindustani is entirely natural. In the same way Persianized Urdu is unnatural and artificial.

... Many painful memories come to my mind but I do not like to recollect them.

I do not at all like this quarrel over the name. Whatever may be the name, its activities should do well to the entire country or the nation. We should not squabble over a name. Is there any Indian whose heart will not exult after listening to Iqbal's "Sare jahan se achchha Hindostan hamara"? If there is any, I will consider him unlucky. Should I regard these lines of Iqbal as Hindi or Hindustani or Urdu? Who can say that it is not the national language or that it is not sweet or that it does not express maturity of thought? It may well be that today I am alone in my view but it is clear that neither Sanskritized Hindi nor Persianized Urdu will win. Victory will go only to Hindustani. We shall forget this artificial quarrel and feel ashamed of it only when we forget our internal jealousies". (https://gandhiking.ning.com/profiles/blogs/thaughats-of-mahatma-gandhi-on-national-language-1

language?" is a question that Mahatma Gandhi delved into deeply while advocating the cause of Hindustani proposing five simple qualifiers:

> (1) For the official class it should be easy to learn.
> (2) The religious, commercial and political activity throughout India should be possible in that language.
> (3) It should be the speech of the majority of the inhabitants of India.
> (4) For the whole of the country it should be easy to learn.
> (5) In considering the question, weight ought not to be put upon momentary or short-lived conditions.[7]

It is another matter that the Indian Constitution had endorsed Hindi in Devanagari script as one of the official languages of the nation, alongside English, and not a national language, owing to the opposition of non-Hindi-speaking states, primarily of the south, and even after 15 years of its implementation, when its position was reviewed, in order to declare it as the sole official language, the spate of protests in 1965, stalled the process. The contention between national and nationality languages, as most regional languages of the country lays claim to being a nationality language, does not seem to be one that has any easy resolution in the offing. The writings of Premchand on the question of national language that falls in the period between 1931-1936 remains to be of topical interest as it not only addresses the issue of conflict between the Hindi and Urdu variants of what he, like Gandhi, conceived of as 'Hindustani,' he also took the concerns of the various dialects of Hindi—*upabhashaons* or 'sub-languages'—seriously, and pitting these against his concern for the development of established as well as developing regional languages, his advocacy of translating literature produced in other Indian languages into Hindi and from Hindi, into other regional variants, calls for a protracted, democratic vision

7. 'Hindi: The National Language for India'; *Speeches and Writings of Mahatma Gandhi*, pp. 395-99; 20-10-17. (https://www.mkgandhi.org/towrds_edu/chap15.htm)

that has nothing to do with any kind of fundamentalism, other than a genuine concern for a national language and a national literature that could demonstrate the diverse and varied heritage of this subcontinent. Advocating for the cause of Hindustani and later Hindi as a common language to be used for official purposes in place of English, campaigning for Hindustani as 'rashtrabhasha' or national language as it was spoken and understood by common citizens, peasants and workers along the length and breadth of the country led to the vision of promoting it as a national language that could give shape to a national literature as well, was not an ill begotten notion. Its rivalry with English and the claim of English to be a world language, not to mention the capital investment by the British Council alone in promoting English in India even in the twenty-first century, presents a chequered narrative of opportunities and challenges that has remained as spurs igniting debates on the issue of having Hindi (and not Hindustani) as the sole official language in India.

Anuradha Ghosh

Rashtrabhasha

1. Special Issues in Urdu (*Urdu ke Visheshank*)

The Urdu magazines have also begun the practice of bringing out special issues. *Nairange-Khayal, Saki, Rehnuma-e-Taleem,* and others have come out with beautiful illustrated editions. The *Rehnuma-e-Taleem* special issue is so prodigious, it is unlikely that a volume of such density might have been published in any other language in India. It comprises of about 800 pages and has more than 200 pictures. The Hindustani Academy too has begun to release a quarterly pamphlet named *Hindustani* and our friend Shri Sudarshan ji has also launched an illustrated magazine called *Chandan*. After this, *Sitara, Filmistaan,* and other magazines are also being published, and they are mainly concerned with the subject of cinema. As far as I know, there has not been any cinema-related magazine in Hindi yet. In this matter, Urdu has outdone Hindi. Though among these filmy magazines there isn't any of high quality yet; however, now when the work has started, it will also be completed some day. Witnessing such lassitude in Hindi, we are compelled to feel dismayed.

[Editorial, *Hans;* February 1931]
Translated by Trisha Lalchandani

2. The Need for Literary Clubs (*Sahityik Clubon ki Aavashyakta*)

The number of speakers and writers of Hindi in India is not

less than 15 crores.[8] Those who speak and understand Bangla are about 5 crores in number. Despite that, the consumption of Hindi books is insignificant in compared to the consumption of Bangla books. Here, the best magazines incur losses and the best books lie rotting in godowns. When a gentleman buys book, then the entire neighbourhood scrambles after it. People run a mile or two for it. Often, the owner of the book does not get to see it, as it changes hands quite swiftly. Witnessing the situation, he thinks to himself, 'what soup have I landed myself in?' If one doesn't lend the book, then one is given the titles of being hard-hearted and selfish. If they lend it, the book does not come back. Hence, why order books at all? This is our love for literature! We want to read books, but not by spending our own money. Even those who have an adequate income are not shy of begging for books. If this situation continues, then I do not understand how any progress can be made in literature. Publishers enter the field with great enthusiasm but in a year or two, they withdraw after having spent even their domestic savings. New magazines keep getting published every day and, exterminating five or ten thousand rupees, make their exit. The cure for this tardiness lies in the opening of new literary clubs. Such clubs must be established in every town and village. In the cities, it is mandatory to have such clubs in every locality. If even one or two enthusiastic gentlemen take courage, they will find ten, twenty, perhaps thirty such lovers of literature who would give them 4 *annas*[9] every month with joy. If, through these clubs, books and magazines worth an annual subscription of Rs. 100 is ensured, then rescuing literature may be possible. Even if ten thousand such clubs are established in the entire country, some good will come of it. One of the tasks that the members of these clubs will have to undertake is motivating lovers of literature to buy books worth one, two or four rupees a year in a regular manner. In developed nations, such clubs make a great effort and this is

8. 1 crore equals 10 million.
9. 1 anna used to be 1/16th of a rupee.

precisely the reason why even ordinary books sell up to fifty thousand in number there. I hope that the Hindi world will give it the attention that it deserves.

[Editorial, *Hans*; June, 1931]
Translated by Trisha Lalchandani

3. The Plague of the English Language (*Angrezi Bhasha ka Rog*)

I have drawn the attention of the readers of *Hans*[10] to this issue earlier too. I am pained as I write this that even our activists, working at the national level, are as much afflicted by this disease, as the employees of the government sector, or lawyers, or college teachers. There is no doubt that they have started wearing *khaddar*,[11] however, there is not a trace of either tradition or culture in their mindsets. If you go to a committee meeting, you will find *khaddar*-clad gentlemen rattling away in English. The words and sentences that they have read in the dailies or the English newspapers are impatient to come out and at the very first instance, they sprout forth. It is comical when these gentlemen refuse to desist from conversing in English even in front of women

10. The Hindi literary magazine *Hans*, edited by Munshi Premchand was first published from Benaras in 1930. This magazine which Premchand edited till 1936 was a shaping influence on Hindi language and literature. The magazine continued to be brought out by the celebrated Hindi author Shri Jainendra Kumar and Premchand's wife, Shrimati Shivrani Devi. The editorship was then taken up by Shri Shivdan Singh Chauhan and Shri Shripat Rai and subsequently by Shri Amrit Rai (noted Progressive Writer in Hindi and son of Premchand) and then by Shri Narottam Nagar. In 1959, a special issue was jointly edited by Shri Balakrishna Rao (All India Radio, Broadcasting Division who was responsible in organising popular programmes to promote Hindi as a national language) and Shri Amrit Rai. It was then published in Delhi from 1986 to 2013 under the editorship of Shri Rajendra Yadav, a well-known writer and critic in Hindi.
11. Khaddar or khadi is Indian homespun cotton.

who do not know the language. Until when will this spell of the English language hang over our heads? Until when shall we be slaves of the English language? What spills forth from this is that nationalism has not permeated the depths of our hearts. Except Mahatma Gandhi, we do not see any other leader stress on the campaign for the Hindi language. Let this be understood that until our national language is established, the creation of the Indian nation-state will only be an idea and a dream. The Japanese express themselves in Japanese; the Chinese in the Chinese language; the Iranian people in Persian; but the educated people of India are proud to read and speak in English. There are many men who do not hesitate in saying that they find it difficult to write or speak in Hindi. This is a simple and straightforward instance of intellectual servitude. Even the most accomplished Indian speaks to an Englishman in English. That the English should speak to him in Hindustani does not occur to him at all. Anyway, speaking to an Englishman in English can be excused but there is no reason to speak amongst each other in English.

[Editorial, *Hans*; September 1931]
Translated by Trisha Lalchandani

4. India's National Language (*Bharat ki Rashtrabhasha*)

In a lecture given at the '*Angrezi Bolo*'[12] Union, India's former Viceroy Lord Reading[13] expressed his sheer satisfaction, pleasure and pride since some representatives present at the round table were extremely competent, by virtue of the fact that they were proficient in English. When the Viceroy Lord Reading was in India, it gave him immense pleasure to see the publicity and privilege that the English language was enjoying in the country. He says, "English is the national language of India. It is the language of peace, harmony and order." The greatest of scholars have not been able to resolve the question

12. 'Angrezi Bolo' means 'Speak English.'
13. Lord Reading was the Viceroy and Governor-General of India from 1921 to 1926.

as to 'what is the national language of India?' After much deliberation 'Hindustani' has been declared as India's national language. Even the greatest of English scholars do not go so far as to declare English as India's national language. In our opinion, the Viceroy was a little too quick to decide our national language for us. What took a beating was the capability of the natives. All colonised countries eventually adopt the language of the colonisers. If a Bengali brings home a pet parrot, the bird's mother tongue inevitably becomes Bangla. Perchance the offspring of that parrot is adopted by a Hindi speaker, it acquires Hindi as its mother tongue. Some parrots tend to forget their own language to such an extent that they forget how to chirp. Likewise, some belonging to the new breed of Indians have forgotten Hindi to such an extent that the letters they address to their parents also get written in English. It is common for foreign-returned Indians to pronounce '*tum*' (तुम, you) as '*tum*' (टुम). Even in matters of language we Indians have become such slaves of the British that other extremely rich and beautiful languages are overlooked by us. For instance, French is a far more sweet-sounding, expressive, and widely accepted language than English. It is popular not just in Europe but many other regions of the world. We come to know of this only after we leave England to go somewhere else; and there, if we only know English, then we are considered foolish. English is, no doubt, a very rich language, but the extent and manner in which we have submitted to its supremacy is a matter of little pride.

What remains is the question of "the language of peace, harmony and order." We encounter examples of this almost every day. Newspapers such as the *Daily Telegraph*, *Daily Mirror* or *Daily News* (all three of which are from London and are the chief newspapers of the conservative wing) are all printed in English, yet the leaders of England's politics are mostly controlled by them, and their language is extremely acerbic, venomous, spiteful and derogatory.

[Editorial, *Jagaran*; 5 December 1932]

Translated by Sarah Mariam

5. Hindi in the Baroda State (*Baroda Rajya mein Hindi*)

Baroda is one of the most developed and well-governed states in Hindustan (India). In matters of social reform, Baroda has been ahead not only among the princely states but in all of British India. Compulsory and free education and the abolition of child marriage are among the many reforms undertaken there. The most recent is the granting of permission to the untouchables for unhindered entry into any temple across the state. This has certainly saddened some of the orthodox, social purists[14] present there. The impact of this move is far-sighted and favourable. The next immediate task of this state is to accept Hindi as the state language. Among the ones under the British, the central provinces were the first to bring in this reform by declaring Hindi to be the court language. After this, Baroda would perhaps be the first such state of great importance where Hindi would be dominant. Baroda is a Maratha state where most of the residents are Gujarati. It is for this reason, that this reform has an even greater importance. Should we now expect that Alwar, Bikaner, Udaipur and other non-Maratha states will also replace Urdu with Hindi at the helm of affairs?

The Baroda government too has committed many mistakes, among which the greatest was to discontinue the pension of the senior gentleman Abbas Tayyibji.[15] How silly it is that the retired pensioners of the Indian Civil Service can daringly take part in the movement against the Indian government, while a great servant of India receives no pension from one of its princely states.

[Editorial, *Jagaran*; 5 December 1932]
Translated by Suvankur Sukul

---

14. In the original, the term used is *'samajik kitanu'*, which literally translates as 'social germs'.
15. Abbas Tayyabji (1853-1936) was the first Indian barrister at the age of 21 and went on to serve as the Chief Justice of the Baroda High Court.

6. Debates on Hindi in Hindu Universities (*Hindu Vishwavidyala mein Hindi Vaad-Vivaad*)

Last Sunday, there was a debate in Hindi in the Kashi Vishwavidyala (University of Kashi). Apart from local colleges, students from Jabalpur, Patna, Gurukul Kangri, etc., had also participated. The topic of the debate was: Hindi language as the sole medium of nation-building. The chairperson of the local council, Sir Sitaram, was the chief judge for the event. Four female students of the local colleges also participated. The attendance was good. Around 25 students participated in the event; the majority of the students' presentations reflected their personal view points. Only a few students paid attention to the essential elements of repartee and critical arguments during the rebuttal round of the debate. It is essential for nationalism to have caste, religion, geo-political situations, culture and language as its components; but in my opinion, having one language is the most important factor for nationalism. Without a national language there cannot be any notion of a nation. Wherever there is a nation, there has to be a national language. If the whole of India has to be made one nation then it has to base itself on one language. Usage of the English language is merely circumstantial; we cannot give it the status of a national language. It is language which creates a nation, its literature and culture, and also establishes its ideals. The obstacles that the rivers and mountains used to create in the growth of nationalism have started being wiped out by railways and airways. A nation cannot be stable if despite having a culture of its own, it does not have a national language. Sometimes disputes amongst people speaking a common language leads to the creation of separate nation-states. The United States of America is an example of this. But it is the only example of this kind. As opposed to this we have examples of various nations having one breed, one culture, and one religion. This only proves that the role of language is the most important to the process of nation-building. Even the German philosopher, Fishe, has given primacy to language. In this debate, presentations of two of the students of Gurukul Kangri were the best and were awarded trophies. We congratulate these students on their success.

[Editorial, *Jagaran*; 26 December 1932]
Translated by Saroj Kumar Mahananda

7. Higher Education through Hindi (*Hindi dwara Uchch Shiksha*)

On the auspicious occasion of the convocation at the Kashi Vishwavidyalaya (University of Kashi), Mahamana Pandit Madan Mohan Malaviya[16] supported the use of Hindi as a medium of instruction and said that very soon Hindi will be introduced up to intermediate classes in colleges. The Hindu University should have taken the lead in this matter and we are happy that the university has lived up to our expectation. We all have a fair amount of experience about how education through English wastes so much of students' time. Students are even compelled to rote-learn subjects like History and Geography and their entire energy is spent on understanding the language; they have no opportunity to pay attention to the subject matter. This drawback can be overcome by replacing it with the medium of Hindi. It is possible that due to this reform students' hold on English might not remain the same or they might not be able to speak or write as fluently. Many of our affluent persons are so enamoured of English that they send their children to English schools only. These people may not like this reform, but since it is proved now that the market value of education is gradually decreasing, then why should language be the cause for jeopardising the career of students? After all, in countries like Germany, France, Japan and others, education is imparted through their national language. Don't they produce people who can speak and understand English?

[Editorial, *Jagaran*; 26 December 1932]
Translated by Saroj Kumar Mahananda

---

16. Mahamana Madan Mohan Malaviya (1861-1946) was an educationist and served twice as the President of the Indian National Congress.

8. Propagation of Hindi in the South (*Dakshin mein Hindi Prachar*)

The propagation of Hindi in the provinces of Madras and Andhra is being carried out in such an organised and satisfactory way that it is praiseworthy in all respects. At this time, there are nearly three hundred promoters working permanently in different centres there. The 'Pracharak Mandal' (the leading group of activists for promoting Hindi) publishes a useful monthly magazine called *Hindi Pracharak*; every year a "Pracharak Sammelan" (Promoters Conference) takes place, and through this, it conducts three examinations called "Prathamik" (Elementary), "Madhyama" (Intermediate) and "Rashtrabhasha" (National Language), the popularity of which can be estimated by the number of people who sit for the examinations. This year, there were 2504 candidates at the "Prathamik" level, out of which 2159 sat for the examinations and 1816 passed. At the "Madhyama" level, 1149 took the examination, out of which 741 passed. 579 had taken the examination at the "Rashtrabhasha" level and 342 have passed. The total number of candidates was over 4000. The number of examination centres was 281, out of which 175 were in the Andhra province, 19 in Tamil Nadu, 52 in Kerala, 34 in Karnataka and 1 in Mumbai. The progress of the campaign for the spread of Hindi can be measured by the fact that last October, the number of participants had doubled to that of the number recorded the previous year around that time. And the influential, well-known gentry of that province were also involved in this enterprise. Among them Sir C.P. Ramaswamy,[17] Diwan Bahadur V.S. Subramaniah Iyer,[18] Justice A. Venkatrao et al are also present. On seeing the arrangements made for the programme of the "Hindi Premi Mandal" (Circle of Hindi

17. Sir C.P. Ramaswamy (1879-1966) was a lawyer, administrator, and a politician; he served as the Advocate-General of Madras Presidency.
18. Diwan Bahadur V.S. Subrahmaniah Iyer (b. 1877) was the Divan of the Travancore State from 1929 to 1932.

Lovers), it can be understood how diverse their interests and how noble their intentions are:

1. Arrangements for meetings, festivals and social gatherings;

2. Education in the Hindi classes;

3. Preparing students for the examination conducted by the Prachar Sabha;

4. Promoting Hindi in the local schools and colleges;

5. Performing Hindi dramas in order to promote love for Hindi among common people.

We heartily congratulate the Hindi-lovers in Madras for their enthusiasm and effort. Indian nationalism depends on a national language and the Hindi-lovers of the south, by spreading Hindi in the region are working as builders of the nation. It is impossible to conceive of a nation without a national language. Where there is a nation, there ought to be a national language. If the whole of India has to be constituted as a nation, it has to have one language as a foundation. The use of English is contingent; we cannot designate it as the national language. It is language that builds a nation, its literature and culture, and creates values. In spite of uniformity in culture, if the basis is not a national language, the nation cannot sustain itself.

[Editorial, *Hans*; December 1932]
Translated by Suvankur Sukul

9. Old Urdu (*Purani Urdu*)

The Hindi world is familiar with Insha's *Ketaki ki Kahaani* (The Story of Ketaki).[19] Insha was born in the eighteenth century. The seeds of Urdu were however sown much before his arrival upon the scene. The first writing in Urdu was done in the reign of Qutubshah of the South—the emperor of Golkonda at the beginning of the seventeenth century. It is interesting to note that even though Urdu germinated in North India, the earliest writing in Urdu appeared in the Southern part of

19. *Ketaki ki Kahani* is considered to be the first prose piece in Hindi.

the country. Here is a specimen of the Urdu that was in use at that time:

> The king hosted a soiree one night,
> The ministers' sons graced the occasion with delight.
> Each one so handsome, so lovely of face,
> Each one so pleasant, and so full of grace.
> Holding their carafes, their goblets in hand,
> The listeners would fall into an ecstatic dance
> The singers sang with such romance,
> That the listeners were sent into a trance.
> When the musicians began to sing,
> The world began to dance and shake
> The songs they played won the king's heart,
> And another array of melodious ragas would start.
> The *ragas* and tunes they presented in praise of the king,
> The wine, the goblets, the sweets, condiments and the carafes,
> Left the people present intoxicated.

Prior to Qutubshah, Mohammad Kuli Qutubshah in the period 1581-1611 wrote a *masnavi*[20] in Urdu. He is probably the first person to have composed poetry in Urdu. Here is a specimen of his composition[21]:

> *Te-se, haatan mate-haath mein, bataan mate-baat mein,*
> *Ghaat-tarah, athe-the, haur-aur.*
> Focusing on the young, dusky girl,
> He has lost all his senses and become oblivious.
> Looking at her cypress-like stature,
> Her refulgence to me was like the refulgence of the moon.

---

20. *Masnavi*, also known as *mathnawi*, is a series of distichs/couplets in rhymed pairs that makes up a characteristic type of Persian verse, used chiefly for heroic, historical, and romantic epic poetry and didactic poetry. (https://www.britannica.com/art/masnavi)
21. The source text as found in the texts edited by Ram Vilas Gupt as well as Ramvilas Sharma does not match in entirety with the text available in Mohammad Kuli Qutubshah's *Qutubshah* in the Urdu original. Lines 1, 2, and 5, are nearly senseless, in that they are a stringing together of words which do not make a meaningful whole, and therefore have been left untranslated.

Chhand-chaturai, saun-se, disan-dikhai dena.
Every part of their bodies shook in anger
And their stone-like hearts turned to water,
Each of them was like a mountain or a tower,
Countless people died with their mace.
As they resolved to fight in a brave manner,
The world turned upside down,
An uproar was heard, "kill them, kill them,"
Doomsday became apparent on the earth.

Sense: The hearts of the grand mountains burst and turned to water when the armies were enraged. Every soldier/warrior was like a mountain, bearing a lethal weapon in his hand. As the valiant warriors proceeded to the battle-grounds, they marched ahead with heads held high, crushing the world under their feet.

As the river of blood began to overflow,
The skies began floating on it like a boat

In those days, the word'gagan' was also used in Urdu.

[Editorial *Hans*; December 1932]

Translated by Sarah Mariam

10. The Third Conference of Campaigners for Hindi in South India (*Triteeya Dakshin Bharat Hindi-Pracharak Sammelan*)

National language might not be the most important factor determining national unity, but it is definitely important and it is also certain that besides Hindi, no other regional language can claim to be the national language of India. Therefore, from the perspective of national integration, the spreading of Hindi in south India is a huge task. Hindi Prachar Sabha (Association for Campaign of Hindi) has its own institute and its own magazine; it conducts many examinations and those who pass are awarded. It also organises an annual conference and recently it held its third conference, where Shri Devdas Gandhi[22] was the chairperson. The lecture delivered by him

22. Devdas Gandhi (1900-1957) was the fourth and youngest son of M.K. Gandhi.

on this occasion was very thought-provoking, inspirational and full of substance. Assessing the work of the organisation, he said:

> The success that you have attained in these 14 years compels me to congratulate you. In this region you have been able to reach fifty-five lakh people, out of which four lakh have obtained a working knowledge of Hindi and twenty-three thousand people have taken your examination. Another significant fact that I am observing is that your work is not limited to the cities, but has also spread in remote places. Among the 285 examination centres of last October, there are more than 200 villages.

Devdasji's suggestion that the men and women of south India who love Hindi should tour north India is universally acceptable. Living together in the northern region for two or three months would not only augment the love and intimacy between people, but would also enable them to be so proficient in the Hindi language that cannot be obtained by years of studying books in Hindi. The labourers of the United Provinces start speaking fluent Bangla in about six months to one year of their stay in Calcutta. The kind of habit of speaking English that can be developed in England, cannot be done in India. We desire that the Prayag Sahitya Sammelan[23] (Literary Conference) and Nagari Pracharini Sabha[24] (Society for Promotion of Nagari) also contribute to this work of Hindi Prachar Sabha of the south and on their own expense send ten or twenty Hindi workers to the south every year.

To expect anything from the government regarding the spreading of Hindi is to depend too much on it. But it is regrettable that the regional scholars and leaders have been indifferent to this issue until now. We do not claim that Hindi is a supremely developed language. The ancient literature

23. Hindi Sahitya Sammelan Prayag was an institution established in 1910 to promote the Hindi language and literature.
24. Nagari Pracharini Sabha was an organisation founded in 1893 in Varanasi to promote the Devanagari script over the Kaithi script.

of this language can claim equality to any of the ancient literature in the regional languages, but modern literature in Hindi is still lagging behind the modern literature in many other regional languages. But the claim of Hindi is not based on its literature, rather it is based on its comprehensiveness and lucidity. And in this regard, no regional language can match it. If Hindi had received the same encouragement in other provinces as it has in south India, by now it would have been used on a much larger scale. If the use of Hindi is made compulsory in the schools of other provinces, then the issue of national language would be easily resolved.

In these invaluable terms, he has discussed how bright the future of the Hindi language is and how its propagation would strengthen nationalistic feelings:

> Every kind of enemy of India has a genuine fear of Hindi. Those who doubt this can clear it by observing the work going on in south India. Wherever Hindi works as a shelter, the divides between Brahmin and non-Brahmin, literate and illiterate, city-dwellers and villagers, old and young have collapsed. Along with the propagation of the language, genuine unity has begun to be established. It is in fact surprising why it took so long to launch this movement for one language. But the one who is faithful does not regret the past. He is only mindful of the present. Keep faith, the future is bright indeed.

[Editorial, *Hans*; January 1933]
Translated by Suvankur Sukul

11. The Appeal of the *Hindi-Gyan-Yatri-Mandal*[25] to Hindi-Speakers (*Hindi-Gyan-Yatri-Mandal ki Hindi-bhashiyon se Appeal*)

We publish this appeal with immense pleasure and request all Hindi-lovers to encourage and support the Hindi Gyan Yatri Mandal:

> It has been almost fifteen years since the Hindi Prachar Andolan (Campaign for Promoting Hindi) was initiated in South India.

25. Society of Hindi Knowledge Seekers.

At this time there are around four hundred Hindi Prachar Kendras (Centres for Learning Hindi), where, so far, more than six lakh men and women have studied Hindi. All the credit for the success of this movement goes to venerable Mahatmaji. It is possible that this work may be perceived as satisfactory from the perspective of being in an early stage of the campaign. However, those Hindi-lovers who earnestly believe national language to be the essence of national life, may hardly be content with this. It is said, that the Hindi Prachar Andolan has two most important aspects; they are the national and the literary aspects. It is worthwhile to record at present, the campaign for Hindi in the south from a nationalist perspective. No attention has so far been given to the literary aspect. It is precisely for this reason that in this long period of fifteen years, the Hindi spoken by South Indians could not become polished, free-flowing and idiomatic. There is a complete lack of appropriate institutions or people here that can pay attention to the literary aspect. At present, out of the three hundred campaigners serving the cause of Hindi in South India, not more than twelve or thirteen are from the north, and among the rest, people with high competence in Hindi can be counted on one's fingers. It is extremely regrettable that neither the educated, enthusiastic youth of north India has paid attention to this, nor the experienced litterateurs here to the South Indians. It is important for Hindi speakers to cooperate with the South Indians not only because of the desire to promote it as the national language but also to preserve the originality of their mother-tongue. In this age of revolution, it is harmful for the country that the speakers of Hindi remain indifferent, and do not harbour productive thoughts about the developments of its possible future.

'Alparambha Kshetrakar' (A small beginning is a safe one). According to this Aryan utterance, in order to do away with this weakness as much as possible, with strong determination an institution for knowledge-seekers, "Hindi Gyan Yatri Mandal", was established here in 1931. The principal of Hindi Pracharak Vidyalaya Madras, Pandit Hrishikesh Sharmaji was elected as the president, whose august presence is the glory of the institution. He is very much in favour of Hindi literature being propagated in the south and it is because of his kind encouragement that every year some Hindi-loving people are taking the examination conducted by the Hindi Sahitya Sammelan (Hindi Literary Conference). Through him the circle has become acquainted with the praiseworthy generosity of many of the devotees of Hindi literature. Respected Acharya Dwivediji Maharaj[26] has kindly described our enterprise as praiseworthy and timely. Hindi Sahitya Sammelan Prayag and a few other institutions promoting Hindi will provide us with the much needed support. The Nagari Pracharini Sabha in Kashi has considered teaching a few South Indian students especially under their aegis. Besides, the widely-respected and experienced Babu Shyamsundar Dasji,[27] Babu Premchand ji, Srinath Singhji, Pandit Haribhau Upadhyayji,[28] Pandit Ramnaresh Tripathiji,[29] Professor Ramdasji Gaud,[30] Pandit Harishankarji Sharma,[31]Professor Indraji, Shri Mohanlal 'Mahato Viyog',[32] Pandit Makhanlalji Chaturvedi[33] et al have promised to be of help in the fulfilment of the objectives of the circle. It is a matter of great joy that owing to the kindness of Babu Sangamlalji Agrawal, MABL, the girl students of South India in 'Prayag Mahila Vidyapeeth' (Prayag Women's School) have received a special stipend.

26. Mahavir Prasad Dwivedi (1864-1938) was a well-known Hindi writer.
27. Shri Shyamsundar Das (1875-1945) was a critic and an educationist working in the area of Hindi literature. He was one of the founders of the Kashi Nagari Pracharini Sabha.
28. Pandit Haribhau Upadhyay (1892-1972) was an activist during the Indian Independence Movement.
29. Pandit Ramnaresh Tripathi (1889-1962) was a poet of the Neo-romantic period of Hindi literature.
30. Professor Ramdas Gaud (1881-19328) was a Hindi writer.
31. Pandit Harishankar Sharma (1891-1968) was a Hindi writer.
32. Shri Mohanlal Mahoto Viyog (1902-1990) was a Hindi writer.
33. Shri Makhanlal Chaturvedi (1889-1968) was a Hindi poet. He was conferred with the Padma Bhushan in 1963 and the first Sahitya Akademi Prize in Hindi in 1955.

We convey our heartfelt gratitude to the above-mentioned luminaries and the people who run the institutions for their timely generosity. We are in dire need of devotees of the Hindi language and institutions promoting Hindi which provide shelter in the form of free education, boarding and lodging to at least two youths from Madras every year; because at this time, there are hundreds of talented but poor Hindi lovers who want to obtain higher education in Hindi, living in North India. The future of the movement to spread Hindi is very bright and there are many who are willing to work for that tirelessly, but the number of educators for these true servants of the nation is not satisfactory. Therefore, we plead with the learned Hindi speakers to support the movement which furthers and promotes the 'literary campaign' of the Hindi language in the South.

[Editorial, *Jagaran*; 1 April 1933]
Translated by Suvankur Sukul

12. Hindustani Academy (*Hindustani Akademi*)

Whenever issues related to money crop up in organisations like ours, our activists start wracking their brains. One group wants their friends and colleagues to get all this money, and the other group tries to draw it towards themselves. The group that gets defeated starts creating a ruckus, questioning the organisation and finding all kinds of faults, real and imaginary of the activists in a leading role. But had they themselves won, then they would not have batted an eyelid; they would have found the organisation completely faultless. But because the right to distribute the fruits is not in their hands, they start seeing only faults and drawbacks in the functioning of the organisation. The Hindustani Academy is an organisation of this kind as well. The work that so far could not be done by anyone—which is to keep each and everyone happy—is something that the Academy, even if it desires to do so, would never be able to accomplish. We have carefully read both the letters on such an issue—one written by Rai Sahab Shyamsundar Das and the reply to it, by Sriukt Tarachand Mantri—and we have learned only this that Rai Sahab's criticism was much like those that were generally done with reference to similar matters in almost each and every organisation. Rai Sahab could have been far more critical in his review of the organisation that he considers to be an ideal one, in which he himself is the chief decision-maker. Yes, if Rai Sahab had given instances of how the working committee of the Academy had given awards to certain literary texts, had published some useless book, had arranged lectures, contrary to the literary committee's views, but in his criticism no such examples are cited. As far as the contention that the Academy is not very popular, its books and journals do not sell well, is a totally baseless complaint. Though the Academy is a governmental or semi-governmental organisation, it cannot attain such popularity which other literary organisations can achieve; but we still feel that if the Academy makes an adequate effort, and uses its official position, then its publications can sell well. But do books on serious subjects ever sell like hot cakes and do serious journals and periodicals ever run on profit? If we take profit as the main criterion then out of hundred, eighty of our magazines and journals will have to be closed down. And the Academy is not a business enterprise.

[Editorial, *Jagaran*; 10 April 1933]
Translated by Anuradha Ghosh

13. Quarterly or Trimesterly (*Timahi ya Trimaasik*)

Last Sunday an interesting debate ensued upon the usage of the word *'timaahi'* at the Hindustani Academy. Babu Shyamsundar Das contended that the two words *'timaahi patrika'* went together like chalk and cheese. One Muslim gentleman argued that the word be entirely excluded from the vocabulary and be replaced by the word *'sehmaahi'*. These bright minds fail to understand that the Hindustani Academy does not function as Hindi or Urdu Academy. Its very nomenclature is explicative of the fact that the Academy favours neither Sanskrit nor Persian. The goal central to the Academy is the establishment of a national language—a goal that will be achieved only when we set aside our biases towards Hindi and Persian and embrace the prevalently used words in each language of India. For the purposes of the former we have Nagari Pracharini Sabha for Hindi and Anjuman Taraqqi-e-Urdu[34] for Urdu. The pandits can have their *Tadit Samachaar* and *Vaashnaay*, while the public continues to demand their *Taar* and *Railgaadi*.

[Editorial, *Jagaran*; 13 November 1933]
Translated by Sarah Mariam

14. The Need for a School of Hindi Literature (*Ek Hindi Sahitya Vidyalaya ki Zarurat*)

Hundreds of young men have started coming to Allahabad and Kashi to improve their knowledge of Hindi literature since the campaign for promoting Hindi has gained momentum in the province of Madras, but there is no such institution here which can cater to their needs. There is Deen Sahitya Vidyalaya in Kashi but owing to non-availability of funds it is not in a well-maintained state; its Manager looks after it according to his convenience and whatever he does is mere face-saving. It is not as if he has signed a contract to propagate Hindi and hence all responsibility should be thrust on him. The Hindi Vidyapeeth of Allahabad is also in a similar state. There is provision for teaching literature in the universities, but what benefit can such students get out of it? This provision is only for the students of the university. There is a requirement of such schools where regular classes are held by learned teachers of Hindi and where there is accommodation facility for the students. Having a few scholarships for the students would be even better. Every other day, a new high school

34. Anjuman Taraqqi-e-Urdu was an organisation founded in 1903 in Aligarh with the aim to promote Urdu language and literature.

opens here, which is neither needed now nor has any utility. If only the attention of some benefactors is drawn towards this matter, if this matter is raised in the Delhi Sahitya Sammelan and the need for such schools is proven there, it is possible that wealthy people will take note of it. If such a school is opened in the Hindu Vishwavidyalaya, then it will meet such an urgent need. Isn't it a matter of shame that in a prime centre for Hindi there is no school where higher education in Hindi literature could be imparted? And yet we want to make Hindi the national language! If all the interest in Hindi, raised in different regions of the country, dies down due to our inaction, then the dream of a national language will remain shattered for a long time.

[Editorial, *Jagaran*; 25 December 1933]
Translated by Saroj Kumar Mahananda

15. Lady Abdul Qadir and Her Love for the National Language (*Lady Abdul Qadir ka Rashtrabasha Prem*)

God bless Lady Abdul Qadir,[35] who, while presiding over the Women's Society in Calcutta, stressed the need to propagate India's national language. We are completely in agreement with her statement that our national language, that is, Hindustani be compulsorily included in the curricula in all regions of the country. She wrote her speech in Urdu, but very few women present there understood Urdu completely, which called for the need to translate on her part. Hindustani is spoken and understood in most parts of India, whether it is written in Urdu or Hindi. It is being propagated in Madras. The same has started to happen in Mysore. Bengal hasn't yet lent space for such discourses, although numerous Bengali writers are also renowned scholars and writers of Hindi. The editor of

35. Not much is known about Lady Abdul Qadir except that she was born in 1898 in Jhelum. She wrote Urdu fiction, though domestic responsibilities overtook her scholarly ambitions. She served as the President of the Seventh All India Women's Conference, held in Calcutta in 1935.

the magazine *Maya* is a Bengali gentleman. Several Bengali ladies are also skilled Hindi writers, the name of Shrimati Usha Mitra being worthy of mention here. Her stories add to the glory of leading Hindi magazines. How does one envisage the establishment of a nation in the absence of a national language?

[Editorial, *Jagaran*; 1 January 1934]
Translated by Sarah Mariam

16. Urdu in the Kashmir Assembly (*Kashmir ki Assembly mein Urdu*)

In the plan that has been published in the new legislature in Kashmir, special electoral constituencies are not being kept for landlords and moneylenders, and the British government has deemed a second house of the Assembly for the benefit of the landlords necessary. It is a well known fact that in elections it is the wealthy lot such as the landlords who are the benefactors. Conducting special elections for these communities means nothing but giving them the power of election twice. Along with this, the Durbar of Kashmir has taken the decision to conduct all the proceedings of the Legislative Assembly in Urdu, as a mark of respect for the majority. It is mandatory for the members of the Assembly to be proficient in Urdu. The Muslims of Kashmir have immense love for Urdu, irrespective of whether the language is their native tongue or not. Accordingly, the government, keeping to their sentiments, has taken the appropriate decision. Why is the language of the majority not propagated in our Legislative Assemblies as well? Why is it that all proceedings here are conducted in English?

[Editorial, *Jagaran*; 29 January 1934]
Translated by Sarah Mariam

17. The Need for an All-India Literary Organisation (*Ek Sarvadarshik Sahitya-Sanstha ki Aavashyakta*)

There are All-India organisations for science and philosophy, history and mathematics, education and politics in India, but there is no organisation of this kind for literature. Thus, the common masses have no knowledge of the literary progress of other states, nor do those in the service of literature get opportunities to meet each other.

We are familiar with the names of a few artists from Bengal, but we are completely ignorant of the artists of the Gujarati, Tamil, Telugu and Malayalam languages. And what do we even say of English literature? It is through English translations that we have become somewhat familiar with the literatures of even countries like France, Germany, Russia, Poland, Sweden, Belgium, etc. Yet, except for Bangla, we have no knowledge of the progress of other Indian languages. Every regional language holds its conferences separately, and rightly so. Every region has local councils, but for regional literatures, where is the central organisation? In my opinion, one such association is required, and if the Sahitya Sammelan were to establish this, it would be doing a great service to the nation and to Hindi.

The expansion that Hindi has managed to achieve so far, it has done on the basis of its own strength. Hindi is one language that is understood in all big cities of India, even if it is not spoken there. Had English not come in its way, people from different regions would have conversed with each other only in Hindi. In fact they still do so, even if only those who are unfamiliar with English.

The time has now come to bring our cultures and traditions in regional languages in closer contact so that we can create not just a national language, but also a national literature. The literature of each state has its own peculiarities. It is crucial that all these peculiarities get harmonised within our national language, and our literature, moving out of regional confines, reaches a national status. The way we can move forward in this direction with the help and cooperation of the helmsmen of other languages is not possible through any other means. Even though several Bangla and Marathi scholars write regularly writing in Hindi, and one can predict that the scope of Hindi will forever keep expanding, but with the help of such a national literary organisation, we can accelerate this progress.

Recently I got an opportunity to travel to Bombay. There I had the good fortune of talking to the leading Gujarati writers. I got to know how keen they are on an organisation of this kind. In fact I would say that the very idea came from these bright minds, and I would like to request the honourable officials of the Hindi Sahitya Sammelan to effectively bring this proposal into implementation. The dissemination of Hindi is growing all across India. If the Sahitya Sammelan makes arrangements for such an organisation, then I truly believe that writers from other languages will welcome it with open arms, and both the reputation and expanse of Hindi will grow.

It is a fact everyone knows that regionalism is on the rise in India. One of the reasons for this is also that every state has its own literature. It is only through give and take, and mutual debates that the surge of regionalism can be arrested. The creation of nations lies in the hands of their literatures. If literature is regional, then this regionalism will also dwell deeply in its readers. If annual meetings are held among writers of all Indian languages, then, in place of conflict, the sentiment of amiable cooperation will be generated, and it can be said for sure that with literatures coming together, provinces will also move closer to one another. The scholars, whose mere names we are familiar with, we shall be able to see right before our eyes, and be able to directly hear them articulate their thoughts. In good company, many misconceptions and narrow-mindedness will be got rid of. Somewhere else, we are publishing a short description of the world literature organisation called PEN.[36] If even established,

36. PEN., founded in 1921, originally stood for Poets, Essayists, and Novelists.

major languages of the world require such an organisation, is it then not necessary for the regional languages of India to be associated with a central organisation of this kind? The spirit of India is looking up to its writers for giving it an expression; a philosopher can articulate its thoughts, a scientist can advance its knowledge; but its essence, its sorrows, its pleasures, its aspirations, its dreams are for literature to take care of, and this great power is lying entrapped in the confines of regionalism. It is deprived of the fresh air and light that lies out there, and this confinement is an impediment to its growth and intelligence. The currents of nature, moving on their isolated paths, have become narrow and stagnant. By bringing together these currents, we can induce in them a flow of progress and development. This is the fundamental duty of the Hindi Sahitya Sammelan.

[Editorial, *Hans*; February 1934]
Translated by Sarah Mariam

18. Reflection on the 23rd Hindi Sahitya Sammelan (*23rd Hindi Sahitya Sammelan par ek Drishtipaat*)

Like every year, the much publicised Conference got over with great fanfare in the capital city of Delhi, known for its ups and downs. Having seen the proceedings of the four-day conference, an eager onlooker with a sharp mind would immediately like to say, "When the formless God appears in form, all the devotees of God in the world probably face similar disappointment." At the moment, it would be right to comment only this much on the conference through the perspective of the *shastras*. The following lines will be written on the success of the published proceedings; as it is the Hindi world had several preconceptions about it which anyway appeared laughable. But the exhibition of books seems to confirm all those doubts today as the Pataudi House was emptied of the sounds of laughter of its representatives. Whatever it may be, the conference got over: many resolutions were passed and committees were formed; in other words, fortunes were made.

However, it is certain that the spirit of this year's conference did not crave for aesthetic pleasures of the lover-beloved but hoped to awaken the nation struggling to get back on its feet. Each delegate who belonged to the times, wished that Hindi became the language of the entire country as soon as possible. For four days and four nights, through a shower of flowers, auspicious invocations in a haze of gas lights, the conference tried to bring home the point that we develop Hindi at the earliest so that it becomes a powerful medium of expression of every Indian's emotion and intellect. Although the detailed day-to-day description of the conference is being published in the newspapers, this eye-witness account—that again, written in peace—will interest the readers of *Jagaran* the most.

[Editorial, *Jagaran*; 2 April 1934]
Translated by Saroj Mahananda

19. On the First Day (*Pratham Divas*)

The tired delegates, along with well-acclaimed and esteemed people took out a procession according to the notification. Just as Pradhan Mantri (General Secretary) Shri Pattulalji said, the objective of the procession was to go through the main streets of the town to make the ceremonious inauguration of the exhibition a grand event. The poet of poets, Kavivar Ayodhya Singhji Upadhyay 'Harioudh'[37] inaugurated the exhibition. Though, his speech before the inauguration was entertaining, it generated a feeling of 'excessive moralising'. The exhibition was neither like the Wheeler book-stall, nor like the store of the Hindi Pustak Agency (Hindi Book Agency). It was like a small-time museum, which had not been able to open the eyes of the blind Hindi world as much as it did to gather advertisements from book publishers and awaken a sense of proud appreciation in the minds of writers. After the meal, there was a meeting for choice of subject-areas. In this sitting, one could see an after-the-meal gusto that expressed itself in making proposals for resolutions. The session of the main

37. Shri Ayodhya Singh Upadhyay (1865-1947) was a Hindi writer.

conference began after the making of the proposals and their acceptance as resolutions. How is it possible that girls wearing saffron coloured saris, singing auspicious songs, would not be attractive to the volunteers, who expressed as much delight on seeing them come close, like sergeants express in showing warrants? The pictures of former Presidents fixed on the *pandal*, the prominently written ideal sayings and the red and sky-blue flowers on the coats and *kurtas* of the delegates and special invitees, truly impressed one and all. Seeing the presence of one pessimistic viewer might make it seem that the main session was far inferior to even the provincial meetings, but the message in the speeches of the President, the Chief of the reception committee, etc., made it clear that the conference expressed India's age-long desires. The honourable King of Baroda's direction to use one script, Shriman Ghanashyamdas Birla's[38] directive to use Hindi on a wider scale, and the news about enhancing the ambience of the department of examinations, and also the body of the conference, was noteworthy. In the evening, there was a meeting for the selection of subject-areas like the one held in the afternoon. Till 11 o'clock at night, proposals were being made and resolutions were being taken regarding their acceptance.

[Editorial, *Jagaran*; 2 April 1934]
Translated by Anuradha Ghosh

20. On the Second Day (*Doosra Din*)

After a delay of one and a half hours in the morning, the Sahitya Parishad (Literary Council) met. The Chairperson, Shri Makhanlalji Chaturvedi's speech emphasised the reciprocity that existed between literature and national life; he reminded us about the responsibility that literature had and brought to the forefront its true power. Some excerpts from his speech can work as inspiration for present-day literature. After this,

38. Shri Ghanashyamdas Birla (1894-1983) was an Indian businessman. He was a close associate of M.K. Gandhi.

speeches by Premchandji, Naveenji[39] and others took place. These addresses conveyed that literature ran parallel to people's lives and that there was a need to widen the scope of Hindi literature; this was necessary to usher in complete nationalism. At noon, there was a sitting for the choice of subject matter and from 4 o'clock the main session of the conference commenced. It was announced that Shriyukt Jaichand Vidyalankar[40] would be conferred with the Mangalaprasad Award. At night, there was a meeting of the *Itihaas Parishad* (Council for History) in which, there were lectures by the greatest teachers, Mahamahoupadhyaya[41] Gaurishankar Hirachand Ojha,[42] Shriyukt Jaichand Vidyalankaar and others.

[Editorial, *Jagaran*; 2 April 1934]

Translated by Anuradha Ghosh

21. On the Third Day (*Teesra Din*)

A meeting of the Darshan Parishad (Council for Philosophy) was convened under the chairmanship of honourable Shri Giridhar Sharma Chaturvedi.[43] After his long, learned deliberations, several other scholars addressed the Council. The Council for Philosophy in a unanimous voice recommended the study of the subject and decided that literary organisations should get books on philosophy written and published. At noon, a meeting was convened to discuss the selection of subjects and in the evening at 4 pm, the main session was held. Students were awarded certificates, and resolutions were passed in which errors in grammar were considered and Tandonji[44] emphasised the need to work on it. At night, the

39. Shri Balkrishna Naveen (1897-1970), the well-known Hindi writer.
40. Shri Jaichand Vidyalankar (b. 1898) was a historian who founded the Council of Indian History.
41. Titles conferred to scholars.
42. Gaurishankar Hirachand Ojha (1863-1947) was a historian.
43. Shri Giridhar Sharma Chaturvedi (b. 1881) was an educationist who taught at the universities of Punjab, Jaipur, and Kashi.
44. Puroshottam Das Tandon (1882-1962) was a great advocate of

Vigyaan Parishad (Council for Science) met, in which, after the intense, soul-searching Presidential address of Shri Ramdasji Gaur, Shri Dinanaṭhji Chutail and other scholars deliberated on *Vedkaal Nirnay*[45]and other related issues.

[Editorial, *Jagaran*; 2 April 1934]
Translated by Anuradha Ghosh

22. On the Fourth Day (*Chautha Din*)

Early in the morning, there was a meeting of fiction-writers and editors in the Summit. At the meeting of editors, certain significant proposals were passed. Shrimati Kamlabai Kibe,[46] in her capacity as chairperson of the meeting of writers of fiction, delivered a very enjoyable and perceptive address based on her experiences. There were speeches by Premchandji, Srinath Singh, Jainendra Kumar,[47] Makhanlal Chaturvedi and several others. In the fiction-writers' session, Shrimati Ratnakumari Devi's story titled 'Sandesh' was read out. Apart from this, it seemed as though the literary wrestlers had descended on the arena with all their flourishes. At midday, as was the usual custom, there was a meeting for selection of subjects. In the main session of the conference in the evening, apart from the acceptance of proposals, there were lively, scholarly speeches by Sukhdev Bihari Misra, Chatursen Sastri[48] and others. The important blueprint for a fund-raising campaign of five lakhs was accepted and also the invitation from Indore. At night, there was a poetry reading session under the chairmanship of Shri Mahadevi G. Verma[49] (MA). At this gathering there

---

Hindi who established the Mangalaprasad Award in the field of literature through the Hindi Sahitya Sammelan.

45. Puroshottam Das Tandon (1882-1962) was a great advocate of Hindi who established the Mangalaprasad Award in the field of literature through the Hindi Sahitya Sammelan.
46. Shrimati Kamalabai Kibe was a Marathi poet and short story writer.
47. Shri Jainendra Kumar (1905-1988) was a Hindi novelist.
48. Acharya Chatursen Shastri (1891-1960) was a Hindi writer.
49. Shrimati Mahadevi G. Verma (1907-1987) was a Hindi poet who

were many poets and it was attended by almost three to four thousand people. The poems read out by Shri Bachchan,[50] Ladliprasad Sethi (Indore), Rajkumari Chauhan and others were indeed beautiful. The other poets were suitably hooted by the public assembled there. The Kavi Sammelan (Conference of Poets) continued night till 1.30 am.

In this way, the conference ended on a pleasant note. The arrangements made by the members of the reception committee were commendable. The preparations made for the conference were satisfactory. It is another matter that the crowd that gathered in the neighbouring Royal Cinema was far larger than the numbers gathered at the Writers and Editors Summit. The presence of Hindi-loving people in the Delhi gathering however is no less significant; in fact their importance becomes even more crucial in this context.

[Editorial, *Jagaran*; 2 April 1934]
Translated by Anuradha Ghosh

23. A Nation without a National Language (*Be-rashtrabhasa ka Rashtra*)

There was a time when religious integrity was the chief unifying force that held people together. Believers of one faith came together to be a part of several social and cultural issues. Religion was the root of society and culture, life and philosophy. But this new consciousness has removed religion from that high position and language has a crucial role, though not the main one, in the systems that have been established in its place. Today every community has a language of its own. Though America has one national language, yet it has two nations. In South America, several communities speak Spanish and Portuguese, and yet they are different nation-states. The geographical situation has been the main factor in the creation of these nation states as well as their languages; language too

---

won the Padma Bhushan in 1956 and Padma Vibhushan in 1988.

50. Shri Harivanshrai Bachchan (1907-2003) was a Hindi poet who won the Padma Bhushan in 1976.

is fashioned out of this geographical situation. One might say that people living in a certain region use a specific kind of language to communicate in, or it may be said that some natural forces work on their own to create a particular tongue in a region. It is because of this that sometimes dialects change over a distance of five to ten miles (*kos*)[51] but there is a kind of similarity in it, despite the variations in the manner in which one speaks. It is this similarity that gives shape to a language, organises it, and in it, literature begins to be composed. In the course of time, this evolves into the language of a community in the region and the nation. Today Hindi has become the lingua franca of the regions of Bihar, the United Province, Punjab, Almora, CP,[52] Rajputana and others, owing to its universal usage despite the variations in its spoken form. We use Hindi to communicate or write letters to people outside our own regions. If we assimilate Urdu into Hindi—because the spoken forms of the two languages have no difference—then the number of people who speak Hindi is not less than fifteen crores and the number of people who can understand it is far higher. It is surprising why it has not acquired the status of a national language yet. Even a few days ago, other regional languages on the strength of a developed literature in them claimed the status of a national language but experience has now proved that only Hindi has the potential for it. It must be said that we have not paid attention to this issue so far. In South India, the work of promoting Hindi has gathered momentum. If in other regions too, this could be spread, then our goal would have been within reach, but till now our efforts have been limited only to conducting examinations.[53] The organisations that are working on this issue have undertaken the task of composing literature in their hands but they have

---

51. One kos is equivalent to about two miles or about 3.2 kilometres.
52. CP refers to the Central Provinces which comprised of portions of the present-day Maharashtra, Madhya Pradesh, and Chhattisgarh.
53. Examinations as conducted by the Prachar Sabha.

not at all been successful in it because they have not made any literary organisations. They have wasted their time and efforts in trying to look for books of poetic compositions of the past and the ones they have dug out from the graves do not satisfy the needs of the present age. The worthless conflict between Hindi and Urdu has been definitely raised. What was much required is the work of propagating Hindi in different regions like what is being done in South India. What we needed even more was a national language council that had its branches in all provinces. One could have invited prominent litterateurs of every province to that council and requested them to compose literature in it; their advice and help would have not only promoted the national language but would have also created a national literature. For any country, national literature is as important as national language. And literature is an integral component of culture. As one understands, earlier there was no need for a council of this kind, but now people feel that it is required. Now we have understood, that unless we invite prominent literary personalities of different languages to engage with Hindi and organise conferences and conventions, in which intellectuals and writers from all languages assemble to share their talent and experience, we will not be able to build the nation-state. Whatever we have till now is limited to the province and there is no imprint of the nation-state on it. In order to overcome this shortcoming, we need to immediately bring together the literary talents of India. We believe that Indian writers will happily help us with this, as by writing in the national language they will be able to extend their range of ideas. When we have a national language and a national literature, then we will also have a position in the forum of world languages. In the bi-monthly journal *Triveni*,[54] published from Madras, a Bengali intellectual expressed a similar opinion:

Languages of the provinces operate on their own specific

54. The journal Triveni began to be published in December 1927 from Madras.

> conventions of composition. There is no harm in it. But we will never be able to create a national culture in a true sense that is different from the cultures of the provinces, till we take the advice of select literary writers in the country, with responsibility and look for avenues of publication. It is these people alone who can present before us the higher ideals of art.

The Maharajasahab of Baroda in his speech, from the beginning till the end, emphasised on why and how, Hindi should be made the national language. The Maharaja has given Hindi the status of the official language in his state; his words therefore have further significance. But I do not agree with his view that Hindi can become a national language only when it becomes the common language of the people. Learned writers would not like to write in Hindi leaving the language of their provinces. Language can never be a barrier to those who have the calibre to write. A simple language like Hindi will be considered as one's own by the learned in a few days. They may be able to compose good literary pieces in Hindi as well while continuing to write in their provincial languages and this will give them a wider range and scope. Just like a literary composition must be rendered into English or French, so that it can get an entry into Europe, likewise, to appear before the Indian public, a writer must be able to write in Hindi. If we consider it for a moment that literary writers will be prevented to write in Hindi owing to their attachment and affection for their own language, at least they will benefit from the advice and good company of the learned. In such sammelans or gatherings, one indirectly benefits more than directly, as one's perspectives develop, viewpoints change, giving birth to such relationships in front of which uneasy thoughts concerning the province dissolve on their own.

Probably Bharat[55] alone is such a country in the world where there is no national language. Today, apart from a strong centralised rule, is there any other force that might tie

55. Refers to the Indian subcontinent and not the post-1947 political territory of India.

us together in unity? There is no power in religion, it can be found only in the national language.

[Editorial, *Jagaran*; 9 April 1934]
Translated by Anuradha Ghosh

24. The Promise of Hindi (*Hindi ka Dava*)

A nation can only be built on the common ground of one culture. Language and literature are integral parts of culture. Till the time there is one language and one literature, a nation cannot be imagined. Until a nation has a language to propagate its views in, it cannot be called a nation. The reason behind giving Hindi the status of a national language, despite the presence of many developed regional languages, is that it is understood in most parts of India and can be taught easily in any region. While Bangla is a very rich language, it is not understood much outside Bengal. The same is true for Marathi, Gujarati and other languages. Hindi is the only language that has spread to all corners of India. While earlier it had not spread to the South, the campaign for Hindi has now created lakhs of Hindi speakers and users there as well. Undoubtedly Hindi as the national language will be quite different from its regional variants. It would include words and proverbs from the regional languages and may occasionally break the grammatical rules of Hindi. In such a situation, it might bear a minor formal resemblance to the languages prevalent in Delhi and Meerut. Call it Hindi or Urdu, there is barely any difference, save in their written forms. My colleague Arjun has shared his views on this issue:

> In this matter, it suffices to say that Hindi and Urdu are almost similar languages. There is, of course, a difference in script but the choice of script is ultimately a matter of convenience for the learner. Whichever script may be easily learnt in most parts of India will eventually emerge as the script of the nation. The two scripts can also coexist for some time. This is why the proponents of Hindi never make an appeal to displace Urdu from its position and replace it with Hindi. They only want avenues to be opened

up for Hindi in regions where it has not yet found a place for itself."

[Editorial, *Jagaran*; 23 April 1934]
Translated by Rakesh Sengupta

25. Rescuing Sub-languages (*Upbhashaon ka Uddhar*)

One was surprised as well as saddened to see that in certain regions efforts are underway to put life into *upabhashas* or sub-languages. Avadhi, Brajbhasha, Bundelkhandi and Bhojpuri were considered to be a part of the Hindi language, though all these four languages have literatures of their own. The achievements of Avadhi and Brajbhasha in this regard are commendable. Whatever is there in Hindi literature, is available only in these two sub-languages. Does it then mean that we accord the status of language to dialects? If by collecting and compiling these village folk songs, we are able to preserve the literary content in them, then we would like to be a part of this movement. But to spread the idea that literature should be written in Bhojpuri, Tirhuti[56] and hundred other regional dialects and publish periodicals in them, is nothing but a waste of energy. When literature could not be produced in a language which is spoken, understood and written by fifteen crore people even now, how can sub-languages, which are spoken and understood by not more than a lakh do such a wonder?

[Editorial, *Jagaran*; 23 April 1934]
Translated by Anuradha Ghosh

26. Hindi, Urdu, and Hindustani (*Hindi, Urdu, aur Hindustani*)

Prayag's Hindustani Academy has published the speeches of the late Pt. Padmasinghji Sharma,[57] which he delivered in March 1932 in the Academy, in a book form bearing the above title. Sharmaji was not only an eminent scholar of Hindi and

56. Tirhut is the script used for writing Maithili, a language spoken in some states of India and Nepal.
57. Shri Padamsingh Sharma (1876-1932) was a scholar of Sanskrit.

Sanskrit, but also Persian and Urdu; and his speech was made all the more enjoyable as a result of the perseverance and research he had invested in it. In the first part of his speech, he demonstrated that our language used to be called Hindi earlier and till the time of Amir Khusro,[58] the word 'Urdu' was not used at all. Amir Khusro in 'Khaliq Bari'[59] repeatedly used the words 'Hindi' or 'Hindavi'. During the time of the poet Mir, the word 'rekhta' began to be used. The use of the word 'Urdu' is not found anywhere before the eighteenth century. Perhaps the reason for it is that at that time Persian and Arabic words had not infiltrated Hindi all that much. Once Persian and Arabic words started to be found abundantly, Hindi took two distinct forms, and even today the same name has continued. The word 'Hindustani' has begun to be used during the British rule and now it is a synonym of a blend of languages which is used by ordinary people, and in which all those words of Persian and Arabic used in common parlance have come together with great fervour. The newest name for this language is now the 'national language.'

The Persian script has been popular since the time Muslims took over India. Royal edicts, exchange of letters, and so on, and all judicial work used to be carried out in the Persian script. Educated Hindus too would have to learn Persian, and just as today English-educated people exchange letters in English—because they find writing English easier than writing Hindi—in those days for personal matters too, all correspondence was done using the Persian script.

The divide between Urdu and Hindi grammar is growing gradually. The Maulvis haul the grammar towards Persian and the Pandits drag it towards Sanskrit. Citing examples

58. An iconic cultural figure, Amir Khusro (1253-1325) was a Sufi poet and scholar, known for his poetry in Persian and Hindavi.
59. A book written by Khusro compiling the vocabulary of Arabic, Persian, and Hindavi.

from the works of Raja Shivprasad[60] and Maulvi Abdul Haq,[61] Sharmaji has demonstrated that the difference between the grammars of Hindi and Urdu is compelling them to walk in different directions. Maulvi Abdul Haq says:

> The grammar books in Urdu that have existed till today mostly follow the rules of Arabic grammar. Urdu is purely an Indian language, and it is directly connected to the Aryan languages. Counter to this, the Arabic language shares a relationship with the Semitic language family; as a result, imitating Arabic in writing Urdu grammar is not justified in any way. The specialties of both languages are different, which will be made explicit on further deliberation.

It may be gauged through this quotation that in the opinion of Muslim scholars how misrepresented the disparity between the grammars of Hindi and Urdu is and how they want to eliminate it. The words of another Muslim scholar, Maulana Wahiduddin Salim, are worth considering:

> Some of our friends give proof of Urdu being a non-Aryan language in a strange manner; they select a small piece of text from an arbitrarily picked up book and counting the words declare that Arabic words, compared with Persian and Hindi, are greater in number.

However, it is known from 'Farhang-e-Asfia'[62] that in our language, there are more words of Hindi than any other language. And those gentlemen who try to drag our tongue towards Arabic, they err to such a degree that it will alter the constitution of this language.

One of the most complicated problems in our times is the difference that exists between scripts. We have ascribed to it religious and political significance. It seems quite possible that Persian-Arabic and Sanskrit words will diminish in usage

60. Raja Shivprasad (1824-1895) was a writer of Hindi.
61. Maulvi Abdul Haq (1870-1961) was an Urdu scholar and a linguist.
62. Farhang means dictionary, whereas Asfia is the author-compiler of the dictionary.

as the Hindustani language begins to advance progressively, but elimination of the difference of the scripts does not seem possible even in the distant future. If the Persian script has the flaws of deception and imperfection, then it also has a valuable characteristic, which is its flow and fluency. The Persian script is a kind of short-hand, it saves time and space; and in my view, it is this quality that defends it. However, there are plans for development of Semitic languages, wherever they are used in the world. For Urdu too, quite a few scholars have considered a simplifying it, and designing new symbols; they want to pen those sounds for which there are no alphabets at all in Persian, however this deliberation will scarcely be feasible. In the South, Muslims of Malabar, Madras, Andhra, Mysore, and other provinces, use only the regional language. The Muslims of Sindh, Gujarat, Maharashtra, and Bengal also use the script of their respective regional languages. Even in Bihar, the ordinary Muslims use the Kaithi script. The Persian script is used only by the Muslims of North India and Punjab. If, in our *madrasas*,[63] both the Hindi and Urdu languages are made mandatory up to the tenth class then, in my opinion, after some time the educated society will become accustomed to both the scripts, and it will use whichever it finds refined, accessible, and intelligible.

The views of two Muslim scholars have already been put forth on this question. Some other scholars have also expressed their opinion along almost similar lines. The thoughtful ones have written in favour of eliminating the differences in Urdu grammar, style, intonation and so on, and nearly all of them want that Persian and Arabic words should not be added to Urdu in such large numbers. The words of one of the gentlemen are:

> To gain authority over Urdu, the replication of the linguistic styles of Delhi and Lucknow will not suffice, it is also essential that there should be a moderate degree of proficiency in Persian

63. *Madrasa* in Arabic refers to an educational institution where the Islamic sciences are taught.

> and Arabic and good skills in the Hindi language are also acquired. The foundation of the Urdu tongue, as is known, is based on the Hindi language. Its verbs, conjugation, and nouns have been taken from Hindi; consequently, when it comes to the Urdu language, for someone who does not know the Hindi language at all and only rolls the Arabic-Persian wheel, it may be said that he is trying to reach his destination by running his vehicle without wheels.

An opinion similar to this is expressed Maulana Saleem Panipati.[64] He has explained the process which would make Urdu successful and make it Hindustani in the true sense in the following manner:

> ...that if there is an increase in the instances of the Hindu religion, Hindu deities, Hindu history, and Hindu literature, it will not affect our religion or intelligence, neither does anything compel us that we should believe in the existence of these things; in fact, we will have the following benefits as a result of these additions:
>
> 1. We will become more efficient in presenting diverse opinions.
> 2. We will be liberated of the accusation that it is due to religious contempt that we keep away from Hindu literature.
> 3. Hindus will get better acquainted with our literature.
> 4. It would then be appropriate to consider Hindustani as the national language.
> 5. The foundation of the unity between Hindus and Muslims will grow stronger.

Furthermore, Sharmaji has described the affection that the Muslims of the bygone era have for Hindi. He says:

> Renowned Muslims, not only of Urdu, but also of Persian, have written poetry in Hindi. Amir Khusro is considered the father of poetry in Hindustani or Khari Boli. Many of the later Muslim scholars, of which the leading poets are Malik Muhammad Jayasi[65] and Rahim, have also written poetry in Hindi. Mir Ghulam Ali Azad was a connoisseur of Hindi. Syed Rehmat Ullah was also

64. Maulana Saleem Panipati (b. 1867) was a poet and a critic.
65. Malik Muhammad Jayasi (d. 1542) was an Indian Sufi poet, best known for his epic poem Padmavat.

a learned man with an insight into poetry. Syed Ghulamnabi 'Rasleen' has written a book on the *nayika* (detailed description of the heroine) in the form of Urdu *rubais*.[66] Other than 'Rasleen', Madhunayak, Raskhan, Zauki, Jaleel, Mubarak, and others have become well-known poets. The contemporary Urdu poet Hasrat 'Hazrat' Muhani[67] has also created *pada* (songs in praise of God) in Poorvi Hindi, an example of which is as follows:

Having made me love-sick, where have you gone?
Having driven me crazy, having shown me glimpses...where have you gone?
Captivated by the handsome Shyam,
My body blazes all day long,
How dark is the night of disunion,
Full of lamentation, grief, restlessness, and wakefulness.
So says Hasrat, trapped in the malady of love,
I have given all up, be it music or colour.

In the end, Sharmaji has appealed to both Hindus and Muslims:

> The repository of Hindi and Urdu is the result of the hard work of both communities. In their own respective places, both these branches of language have special significance. Both languages have, in their own way, made considerable development. In the reservoir of both their literature, valuable jewels of both languages have accumulated and the process is still on. The Hindiwalas can learn a lot from Urdu literature. In the same way, the Urduwalas can partake of the treasure of Hindi. If both sides come closer to each other, let go of divisive mentality, and meet each other like brothers, then all those misapprehensions which create distance between them will be banished. For this to happen is not too difficult. Only strong determination and courage is needed. Without unity, it will benefit neither the language nor the nation.

[Editorial, *Hans*; April 1934]
Translated by Trisha Lalchandani

---

66. Rubai is a quatrain in classical Arabic, Persian, Turkish, or Urdu poetry.
67. Hasrat 'Hazrat' Muhani (1875-1951) was an Urdu poet and an activist in the Indian Independence Movement.

27. Some Thoughts on the Subject of National Language (*Kaumi Bhasha ke Vishay mein kuchh Vichar*)

Ladies and gentlemen,

All of us are aware of how important the role of language is in the life and success of a nation, and to elaborate upon it would be an insult to intellectuals like you. This two-legged creature became a man the moment he learned to speak. Though all living beings have one language of their own; and it is in that language that they express their joy and misery, their anger and fear, their agreement and disagreement. Many animals make the condition of their hearts and minds known merely through gestures. That he states his emotions and his opinions clearly and elaborately is a position reserved only for man. Language is the foundation of any society. One cannot conceive of a society without language. The climate of a region, its rivers and mountains, its winter and summer, and other seasonal conditions, all of them together contribute to the development of a unique spirit in the living beings of that place, which leaves its impression on the creatures' countenance, behaviour, thought, and feeling; and to occupy themselves, a language and speech is formulated. In this way, language has a direct link with our soul. It can be said that language is the external form of our souls. It emanates from our souls to manifest in our countenance and appearance. Each of its alphabets is illuminated by the light of our souls. As our soul develops, so does our language. In the early ages, people used gestures to communicate, then they used alphabets to express their feelings, it is those very people who write philosophy and recite *shayari* (poetry); when society transforms, our appearance also changes when we leave that place and inhabit different corners of the world. Despite all this, language accompanies us for centuries, and it keeps awakening a feeling of intimacy and closeness in the speakers of the same language. Amongst the many tools of reconciliation that man has, language has the strongest impact in building relationships. Political, professional, or spiritual relationships become weak, sooner or later, and often sever, however the relationship with language does not bother about time and other forces of disintegration and becomes everlasting.

In early times, just like human beings were organised in small social collectives, there were minor languages in circulation. If one is to implore minutely, then there will be a difference in the languages within 20-25 miles. Kanpur and Jhansi share the same border. Only a river separates the two but there is an apparent difference between the language which is spoken in the northern part of Kanpur and the one which is spoken towards the south of the river. In Prayag alone, there are at least ten languages that are spoken. But as civilisation develops, these local languages merge with a provincial language and the provincial language then becomes universal in nature. Brajbhasha, Bundelkhandi, Avadhi, Maithili, Bhojpuri, and several other such offshoots have their origin in Hindi, but just as small streams mingle in a river and lose themselves, similarly these regional languages have become dependent on Hindi and today even a rustic understands Hindi and speaks the language if there is a need for it. But with the territorial expansion of our nation, the need for such a language has arisen which can be understood and spoken throughout Hindustan, which we can refer to as the Hindustani language rather than Hindi, Gujarati, Marathi, or Urdu and which people will speak and understand the same way as an Englishman, a German or a Frenchman speaks and understands English, German or French. We are not against regional languages. You can achieve as much progress as you want with your language. But without a national language as our central support, your national roots will never be strengthened. We regret that we have not given due attention to the national language. All our honourable ministers agree with the need of a common tongue but no one has paid attention to this issue. We are dreaming of creating a nation which is based only on English rule. It is on this uncertain foundation that we are trying to construct national integrity.

If the biggest challenge confronting the nation in the form of having one national language is ignored, then to keep alive the feeling of being a nation, we need to depend on English; without anything to unite us, we will all be scattered and dispersed, and regionalism will gather strength to throttle nationalism, compelling us to return to a dilapidated state that we were in before the coming of the British.

The main reason for this carelessness is the increasing popularity of the English language and a lack of self-respect which does not perceive the shame of this servitude. It is acceptable today that the official language of India is English and that we should know English in order to assist the British in ruling over the Indian people. It has also become necessary to know English in order to be acquainted with the revolutions which keep taking place in the realms of knowledge, talent, and ideas. All the keys to community, fame, and success are in the hands of English and nobody can consider that treasure insignificant. English forms the sole entry point to meet the cultured and civilised community of the world and we cannot shut our eyes to it. However, in the race for wealth and power—a reckless race indeed—we have completely forgotten the need for a national language; and who would have reminded us of that need? There was, anyway, use of English amongst each other, there was not much concern for the public, and all the needs were fulfilled by our regional languages. English took the place of our national language and it still continues to have a hold over it. The terror of the English language is far stronger than that of British politics, trade, and imperialism. We may rebel against British politics, trade, and imperialism but we have hung the English language around our necks like a shackle of slavery. You want self-rule in place of the British rule. You want your trade instead of their trade. However the English language has stamped itself in our hearts. In its absence, our literate society will fall apart. In the ancient times, there was a difference between Aryans and non-Aryans, now there is a difference between supporters of English and its non-supporters. The supporters of English are like the Aryans. Owing to the favours of their masters, they have some authority, influence, and honour in their hands. The non-supporters of English are like the non-Aryans and their only duty is to serve the Aryans and to arrange items for their indulgences and food. This Aryavaad is growing at a rapid pace, exponentially. If, in a hundred years or two it had spread across the entire nation, then we would have said 'please yourself by all means,' it is a foreign tongue, our work is getting done. However, here, there is no possibility of it reaching the people even in a thousand or two thousand years. Secondly, it is distancing the educated from the rest of the masses. In fact, there is a wall that has come about between them. The language of the imperialistic community should after all have some effect of its pride and power. If by studying English, we consider ourselves a part of the community of the rulers instead of the community of the ruled, then it is not surprising that some of the same arrogance, some of the same pride, the feeling of superiority, should arise consciously in most and involuntarily in a few men. The Hindustani gentlemen have a community of their own, their lifestyle, behaviour, attire, attitudes, are distinct from the general public; it is clear that they are a new outcrop. Our Hindustani gentleman does, or is compelled to do, what our British gentleman does. Angreziyat has hypnotised him, there is magnanimity about him, there is utter hatred towards untouchability, he will even eat the leftovers or *joothan* from the Englishman's table like *prasad* from a guru; however there is no place for the people in his magnanimity, as he considers them to be natives. Of course, when he receives a blow from the Englishman then he runs to the people to complain, the same people whom he considered to be natives who could be used at will. If the British rulers give jobs to him, his sons, grandsons, and everyone else, then the fact of his being a Hindustani or a slave will never be realised by him. The problem is that even there, there is no scope. When they receive one blow after another, then that class turns patriotic, becomes an advocate and a leader of the masses, and drawing courage from the backing of the people, he wants to challenge the Englishman. It is then that he realises the absence of a language using which he can reach the masses. The Congress received some fame by appealing to the masses only in that language. In Hindustan, there are about 24-25 crore people who can understand the Hindustani language. Isn't it a matter of concern that he, who claims to be an advocate of the Indian people, cannot speak or understand the language which is the language of 25 crores; though with a slight effort this language can become the language of the entire country, the disease of demonstrating efficiency and expertise in English has spread so much, that all proceedings in our National Assemblies take place in English, speeches are delivered in English, invitations are sent, all reading and writing takes place in English, even in those institutions which call themselves public institutions[68]. In fact, even the socialists and communists who are the special flag-bearers of the masses, conduct all proceedings in English. When the condition of our national institutions is such then how do we complain about the government departments and universities? However, despite a hundred or two hundred years of reading and writing in English, there isn't a single Hindustani writer whose writings in English have been welcomed. We have become so used to the charity of the English language that now we feel troubled when we have to use our own resources to express ourselves. Our attitude has become mostly like that of a beggar who becomes so comfortable in his situation that he does not work even if he gets paid for it. It is true that the Fates above are doing their own work and the people are involved in developing a national language. Their lack of knowledge in English is creating a favourable climate for the development of our national language. The spread of cinema too is helping to resolve this issue as most of the films released are in

68 The source text here is slightly corrupt.

Hindustani. Everyone wants to speak in such a language that is understood by the largest cross-segment of people but when those very people see their own leaders speaking and writing in English, then they, as sympathisers of the national language are deeply shocked and the thought that the national language after all is not such an important matter crosses their minds. When their leaders, whose footsteps they follow, who shape the tastes of people, consider the national language to be so mean that it deserves intermittent praises by them which in turn would inspire people to worship the national language as one does a lifeless icon, then it would consider them stupid. You may hurl people with whatever accusations you like but you cannot take them to be stupid. The scale of understanding that they internalised, may not be used fully by them, but I can wager that in many matters, people have a better understanding than you or me. One of the main modes of promoting national language is the newspaper, but the entire energy of a newspaper is devoted to carrying the speeches of leaders, analysing and explaining, and then translating them, and because the educated segments consider buying and reading such newspapers a matter of shame, such newspapers cannot be promoted and due to the paucity of income generated, such newspapers cannot be made more attractive and appealing for the reader. If the Viceroy or the Governor speaks in English, we have no objection. But to reach out to your own brethren, if one has to translate your views from English, then it reveals a situation of slavery in a country like Bharat which has no parallels anywhere else in the world. The slavery of the tongue is the real slavery. There are such countries in the world who have adopted the language of their rulers but this is because such nations neither had a culture or a civilisation of their own, nor a history or a language that could be considered their own. They were like those children who in a few days time forget their mother tongues and start speaking in a new language. Is our educated Bharat such a child? One does not want to subscribe to this view, though the symptoms of it are evident.

The question that arises here is what would be the form of that national language on which such emphasis is being placed? We regret to say that till now we have not been able to give any specific shape to it and that is so because the people who could have given it a form were, and still are worshippers of English; but its criterion is that it should be understood by as many people as possible. None of our provincial languages fulfil all the required criteria for it. It is only Hindustani that fulfils it, as in my mind, Hindi and Urdu are essentially one language....[69] Urdu is that Hindustani language in which Persian and Arabic words are more, and just like it, Hindi is that Hindustani language in which there are more words from Sanskrit. Just like it is in English, whether there are more words in it from Greek or Latin or from Anglo-Saxon, both remain as English, in Hindustani too, there are words from other languages and this does not make it any different. In our common conversations we use Hindustani. With a slight effort we can use it for all those affairs that deal with the general public. Here I would like to cite one or two examples from an Urdu newspaper to elucidate my view:

> There was once a time when in villages there was no house without a spinning wheel and a grain grinder. Once relieved of the grain grinder and the fire oven, one would spin some yarn on the spinning wheel. Women would pound grain in the grinder and this would keep them healthy, and make their children strong and hardworking. But now the English culture and manners have not only influenced the cities but has made a total transformation of the villages. In place of hand grinders, now machine ground flour is being used. As there are no longer any grain grinders in the villages any more, who is going to sing while working on them? Those who are very poor still continue to use grinders at home to make flour. The time to grind grain is at the crack of dawn. With the onset of evening, grain is kept in the grinder, with the setting of the sun, women start grinding it.

69. The line that follows is corrupt in the source text.

I consider this paragraph to be an excellent example of Hindustani, which would pose no difficulty of comprehension by any Hindi-knowing individual. Now let me present the third extract from Urdu:

> The aim of being faithful was not confined to living individuals alone. It was such a lover, who sacrificed herself like moths drawn not only to a burning flame, but also on flames that were long extinguished. If the savage hands of death snatched her away from her life partner then she would spend the rest of her life in dedication to his memory and his name. After becoming one with the beloved, a loyal and devoted lover would never think of becoming someone else's.

If the first sentence is written like this—'She not only tried being faithful to living individuals,' and in place of '*wafaparast*', meaning faithful, one uses the word '*premi*' meaning lover, in place of '*rafeeq hayat*' one uses '*jeevansaathi*' or life partner, then it would become clearly Hindustani, and no one would have problems understanding it. Now I will cite an example from a passage in Hindi:

> The use of machines render people unemployed and the new innovations increase further unemployment, then the lack of market, increases the overall problem. The problem of unemployment assumes a terrible shape but to top it all, according to the population estimates conducted after every ten years, it is apparent that the rate of population growth is constant. This leads to the increasing wealth of some capitalists and for their comfort and welfare many new items may be produced.

This is an extract from a reputed and established scholar of Hindi in which three words like '*prayog*' or application, '*avishkaar*' or discovery, and '*samasya*' or problem are such that Urdu-knowing individuals would be unfamiliar with. They may be understood by speakers of all the other languages. It is proved from this that with a slight alteration in Hindi and Urdu, we can make them into a national language. We only need to increase our store of words and that too, not to a great extent. Take another example from another write-up:

> In the everyday relationship that we share with our fellow citizens, do you think that it is because of the judges, prison officers and police that *'samaj-virodhi'* or anti-social activities are kept in check? The *'nyayakarta'* or judge is always ferocious as he is crazy about the law. Those who lodge complaints, those who supply information to the police, police spies, and such allied people who wander about the law courts in order to somehow earn their living, do they not spread lawlessness in society? If one reads the reports of court cases and law suits, probes deeply to find out what lies concealed, uses one's analytical intelligence and does not limit it to the external boundaries of the court but takes it within, then whatever you come to know will enrage you.

Here, in place of *'samaj-virodhi'*, meaning anti-social, one uses the phrase *'samaj ko nuksaan pahuchane wale'* or 'those who try to harm society', in place of *'abhiyog'* or complaint, one uses *'jurm'* meaning malpractice or offence, in place of *'guptachar'* or secret agent, one uses *'mukhbir'* meaning informant, in place of *'durniti'* or impolicy, one uses *'burai'* or depravity, in place of *'vishleshak buddhi'* or analytical intelligence, one uses *'parakh'*, i.e. inspection and examination, and for *'parimit'* or circumscript, one writes *'band'*, i.e. locked up or barred, then it becomes simple and lucid and we can call it Hindustani.

From these illustrations and examples it is clear that by increasing the Hindi diction with words from Urdu and the Urdu diction with words from Hindi, one can work it all out. Since Persian and Urdu were court languages some time ago, the currency that Persian words have is far greater than words in Sanskrit. The difficulty that one has in pronouncing words in Sanskrit have already been seen by scholars of Hindi and they have transformed thousands of words in Sanskrit in such a way that it is now easy to utter them. One can cite several examples from Brajabhasha and Avadhi, but one would not like to go into it and waste your time here. That is why one needs to keep the structure of national language such that in place of Sanskrit words that common people do not understand, Persian words, which though are foreign in origin are kept, as they have become so commonplace that it would not be difficult for the general public to understand them. Only those who have read Sanskrit can understand a term like *'abhiyog'*. A word like *'jurm'* is understood even by the uneducated. *'Mukhbhir'* in place of *'guptachar'*, *'burai'* in place of *'durniti'* are simpler words. Those who are advocates of pure Hindi might differ in their opinion on this. But if we want such a national language that is understood by the largest cross-segment of people, then we have no other option, and who does not want that their views are understood by most people, and that they establish an intimate rapport with all? There is one such section among the advocates of Hindi who say that since most regional languages of Hindustan have their origin in Sanskrit, and since they have many Sanskrit words in them, in Hindi too one must incorporate as many Sanskrit words as possible, so that people from different regions do not find it difficult to understand. Hindi does not gain anything by adulterating itself with Urdu. I would like to point out to friends who hold such a view that if one does so then it is possible that people from other provinces would understand your language, but speakers of Hindi will themselves not understand it. It is because common speakers of Hindi use limited words from pure Sanskrit compared to words from Persian. We cannot close our eyes to ignore this truth and after all, what is the necessity to wrangle with it in the name of having a chaste language? It is true that there is some difference between the language that is spoken and the one which is written. The written language always tries to be close to the spoken one. The merit of written language lies in the fact that it remains close to the one that is spoken. The more one veers away from this ideal, the more unnatural it becomes. The spoken language often changes according to situations. In the milieu of scholars [the language that is spoken differs from the language of the marketplace. Some respect should be given to a well mannered and courteous language but not so much that it hinders its promotion. *'Shin'* and *'kaf'* hold Persian words in bondage; but one has to relax its hold when it comes to the question of national language. Even the greatest of scholars of Punjab use 'qa' ('क़') in place of 'ka' ('क'). In my opinion, the most important aspect about language is that, irrespective of the region to which one belongs, most people are able to speak, write and understand it.], such a language will be neither of Pandits nor Maulvis. Its place is between these two. It is evident that writing dexterously in such a language and the development in its diction has a limited possibility now. One, who has command over both Hindi and Urdu, is enticed into writing in a terse and lively manner. The writer does not only want to express the innermost feelings of his mind, but he wants to present it in a proper construction. One should rather say that a writer writes for those who have a refined literary taste and not for the general public. This is just like the trained musician who sings the classical *ragas* to be appreciated by the Acharyas (maestros) of music and is not bothered by the several ignorant listeners who might be in the audience. If we are to promote national language, we too have to suppress a desire such as this. We need to make concerted efforts to develop our language rather than working for improving the dexterity of its written form. Such a language would surely rankle our ears and eyes, as in some places one would witness the union of corollaries, and in other places one Urdu word would stick obstinately amidst those in Hindi much like a swan among crows. Likewise, amidst Urdu, some Hindi words would appear like a lump of salt in a sweet dish like '*halwa*' spoiling the taste altogether, making the Panditji grumble and the Maulavi sahab wrinkle his nose in disgust and there would be a general outcry that our language is being tortured to die a slow death. This is a conspiracy to wipe out Urdu; this illusion has been created to drown Hindi. But we had to embolden ourselves to withstand such allegations. National language cannot be the language of only the elites or the wealthy. It has to be the language of peasants and workers as well. Just as the nation is not constituted of the rich and the elites alone, similarly, a language nurtured in their care cannot be the language of the nation. Considering the fact that languages are created in marketplaces and alleys, not in conferences or meetings, but what we can definitely do in them is to polish them. On the one hand, we fuss over the nation, and on the other, we stand with bayonets to guard our languages, dare someone eye it. We give ample space to Urdu words in Hindi without any trouble. However, Urdu writers do not allow even the most ordinary Sanskrit words to gain entry. They pick Persian and Arabic words, much like Hindi uses Sanskrit. There is an uproar at the slightest hint of rift between the masculine and the feminine gender. The Urdu tongue has become like the mythical bridge of Sirat on which if there is a slight miscalculation, one can lose balance to reach the pits of hell. The biggest problem in the efforts to promote Hindi is owing to the nature of the use of gender in it. We cannot expect the maulvis of Urdu and the pandits of Hindi to go easy in the face of such entrapments; this work belongs to the Hindustani language, that it frees itself from it all. There cannot be a satisfactory answer to why the word 'eye' should be considered feminine in Hindi and the 'ear' is considered masculine.

I am unable to comprehend how the group, which boycotts the language of the people and raises their lathis against them from a distance itself, can become the national institution, and the people, who cannot speak the people's language, can become advocates of the public, irrespective of their professed allegiance to socialism, or communism, or any other label that they might use. It is possible that at the moment you do not feel the need for a national language and you can continue with your work in English. However, if in future, Hindustan has to protect itself from internal conflicts, then we will have to strengthen all those ties which are a part of the nation and in which the status of the national language is neither the highest nor lower than any other language. No one will have faith in your movement for freedom as long as you retain English as the national language. It is not a drive borne out of the soul, but solely a desire to become a martyr of the movement. There are no slogans for victory and neither are there any showers of flowers. However, those who want to see Hindustan as one nation—not because that as a nation it will suppress others, spread different kinds of illusions, pretending to advance the light of knowledge, promote the business of the wealthy and boast about their strength, but so that they create a feeling of sympathy, unity, and compassion and enable us to take decisions regarding our future according to our wishes—it is their duty to help in the development and deliberation of the national language. And everything is in our hands here. We can establish classes for national language in schools. We can make it mandatory for every graduate to speak and write in the national language. We can reserve a column or two for the national language in every journal, be it in Marathi, or Gujarati, or English, or Bangla. We can use the national language in all our platforms. We can converse with each other using the national language. We will not be able to become a nation in the true sense as long as we are happy in our servitude to English. It is also evident that a language cannot acquire the status of being a national language if its use is restricted to a region. National language will be constituted only when the intellectuals of the provinces will lend their support. It is possible that for five to ten years, there may not be any steady form of language; some may move eastwards, some others, westwards; however the storm will settle after a few days, and a lush and tidy field will emerge in place of darkness and clouds of dust. Those who have the power to give life to the dead and to awaken the ones who are asleep will be seen wandering there. Then, we will not have to learn Marathi or Bangla or Gujarati to derive pleasure and benefits from the writings of Tagore,[70] Munshi,[71]

70. Rabindranath Tagore (1861-1941) was a poet, musician and artist from Bengal who won the Nobel Prize in Literature in 1913.
71. This refers to Shri Kanhaiyalal Munshi (1887-1971), a writer and educationist, who founded the Bharatiya Vidya Bhavan in 1938.

Desai,[72] and Joshi.[73] There will be arise of national literature along with the national language, and Hindustani too would sit in the council of other rich and prosperous languages. Our literature, instead of being regional, will become national. The beneficence of the British rule is such that familiarity with our Sharat, Munshi, and 'Prasad' does not match up to even one hundredth degree of our familiarity with writers such as Edgar Welles[74] and Guy Boothby.[75] If Rabindranath Tagore did not write in English, then few men would have been acquainted with him outside the sphere of Bangla. But, how unfortunate it is that no other mind, besides Mahatma Gandhi's, thought of the need for a national language and emphasised it. The work of giving awards and medals for the campaign of the national language, opening schools for it, introducing journals for it, and propagandising the public is the work of the national assemblies. It is difficult for us to live in this world without the consolidation of the form of the nation. It cannot be said with certainty as to which glorious road will lead us to that goal. However, it is proved on seeing other nations with national languages, that language is one of the important things required for nationality, and those who wish to become one nation, must establish a national language. We believe in this reality, but only in abstraction. We do not have the courage to act upon it. This task is of such importance and gravity that for it, it is important to have an All India Organisation, which will understand its significance

72. This probably refers to Ramanlal Vasantlal Desai (1892-1954), a Gujarati writer, who was a recipient of the Ranjitram Suvarna Chandrak in 1932.
73. This probably refers to Umashankar Joshi (1911-1988), a Gujarati writer, who was conferred with the Jnanpith Award in 1967.
74. Edgar Thaddeus Welles (1843-1914) was an American businessman whose father Gideon Welles served as the Secretary of Navy during the American Civil War. It was Edgar Welles who put together his father's diary intitled Diary of Gideon Welles which appeared in 1909.
75. Guy Boothby (1867-1905) was an Australian novelist.

and think of ideas for its campaign and implement them.

The relationship of language and script is so close that you cannot consider only one and leave out the other. Though there may be some regional apprehension, there is no impediment for the languages that have emerged from Sanskrit to write using one script. Earlier too, Swami Babu Sharadacharan Mishra, ran the campaign for establishing a council for script development and initiating a journal, but there wasn't any great benefit from it. Unification in script is not enough for dispelling differences in languages; and comprehending Marathi in the Hindi script is as difficult as it is in the Marathi script. We can continue to write regional languages in regional scripts—there is no opposition to that; however it is a matter of convenience to have one script for the Hindustani language, not because we have a special attachment to the Hindi script, but simply because the popularity of the Hindi script is widespread, and there can be no difficulty in anybody learning it. The Urdu script however is very different from Hindi, and those who are accustomed to the Urdu script cannot be compelled to use the Hindi script. If language can be unified, then the differences in script will have no consequence. If an Urdu-speaking man realises that simply knowing the Hindi alphabet will allow him to read the ideas of Rabindranath Tagore or Mahatma Gandhi, then he will learn Hindi. In the primary schools in UP both the scripts are taught. Every child knows the alphabets of Hindi and Urdu. As far as reading the Hindi script is concerned, no Urdu-speaking person will be opposed to it. It is possible to teach Urdu to Hindiwalas and the Hindi script to Urduwalas by devoting an hour every week in school. On the subject of writing, this issue is not so easy. Despite the flaws of vowels and so on, there is the aspect of pace in it which those who know Urdu cannot abandon, and we cannot hope for those whose history, culture, and pride is secure in the Urdu script to abandon it in the present circumstances. If those who know Urdu can learn Hindi fluently, then its much-needed consequence will be that the maximum number of people will have learnt the script and the campaign for national language will grow rapidly. In course of time, the matter of script will be decided. The one which is more popular will get currency; all others will be left behind. To raise the issue of differences in scripts is to put the cart before the horse. And we have to move ahead with the condition that both Hindi and Urdu are national scripts, and we have the authority to use whichever script we like. Our convenience, our disposition, and our culture will take this decision.

[Speech/article. Welcome address delivered at Rashtrabhasha Sammelan, Bombay, on 27 October 1934. Published in *Hans*, November 1934; and compiled in 'Sahitya ka Uddesh' and 'Kuch Vichar']

Translated by Anuradha Ghosh and Trisha Lalchandani

28. National Language Hindi and its Problems (*Rashtrabhasha Hindi aur uski Samasyaein*)

Dear Friends,

I would like to thank you from the bottom of my heart for the honour that you have bestowed upon me, though I consider myself thoroughly unfit for it. Neither have I read Hindi literature, nor its history, nor do I know anything about its development. A man who does not get overjoyed on getting such recognition is not human. It is quite natural to be overjoyed on getting such recognition. After getting the invitation, I instantly accepted it. I did not want to take the risk of being like people whose habit is to say no to a thing despite their willingness to agree to it. It is owing to my impertinence that I am standing to do the work for which I have no merit, but I am not solely responsible for this kind of thought. People like me will be found all over. You have to save the face of your invitation. Praise whatever rubbish I speak, create the meaning which is not there, salvage from it the literary and spiritual elements—as those who seek, manage to find something.

I congratulate you for what your organisation has achieved in the relatively short period of fifteen-sixteen years, especially because you have achieved these results with your own efforts. You did not seek the government's assistance. This is a reflection of the confidence that you have. It would not be an exaggeration to say that you embody the intellect of the nation. I doubt whether there is such an organisation and such good activists in any other province. The brains that established the roots of the British empire, those who firmly established the English language, those who are and were eminent in English manners and mores, if those people get determined to promote the national language, then what all can happen? And how fortunate it is that those minds that aimed at proficiency in a foreign language, are working hard for the upliftment of the national language today and from that same place from where such mental servitude began, we see the emergence of nationalism. Those people who have outdone even the British in speaking and writing English, so much so that anywhere and everywhere you see editors of English dailies belonging to this very province; if they want, then they can speak and write in Hindi and outdo those who are proficient in Hindi. After listening to the leaders of the campaign last year, I must accept that the process has started. The majority of writings published in *Hindi Pracharak* are written by you and many of us feel jealous due to the use of refined language, clarity and flow in them. And this is when the love for national language has just made its presence felt, and this province does not want to be free from the domination of English. Who can predict what its speed would be at the time when this love becomes all encompassing? The domination of the English language is the most humiliating, the most extensive and the most difficult aspect of our servitude. Nowhere is it seen in its naked form. The English language has become a heavy cross to bear in every aspect of civilised society. If today we can break this domination, then the burden of our servitude will be reduced by half. The kind of discomfort that a fetter causes to a prisoner is caused by no other thing. The prison house is perhaps better ventilated and cleaner than his own house. Even food here would perhaps be better and more delicious than the food at home. Sometimes, of his own accord he would stay away from his family. The only memory of his punishment is precisely the fetter, that never leaves him, whether he is standing or sitting, sleeping or waking, laughing or talking, not even allowing him to harbour false illusions of being free. More than the physical impact of the fetter, it is the psychological impact that one can never overcome. The English language is a fetter of exactly such domination which has captured our mind and heart in such a way that it has even killed the desire for freedom. Our educated society wears this fetter like a garland out of a lack of choice. This is a question of their daily bread. And, besides their daily bread, if they can also get some respect, some honour and some privilege, then what can be said? Every living being desires to be sovereign. The English language has opened up opportunities and our educated community, like a flock of birds, started feeding on the grains strewn all over, and now however hard they try to flap their wings, they cannot attain the freedom they enjoyed. What is ironic is that this flapping of the wings is not to get out, it is only for some entertainment. On top of this, his wings have become lifeless, and it doesn't have the strength to fly; even the belief that foodgrains will be found outside is also not there. Now this is the cage in which they are permanently caught.

But, friends, those days are fast disappearing when a foreign language was learnt to dominate one's poorer brethren. The way in which talent and wisdom have been misused for many centuries, because of which we have established our aristocracy and have separated ourselves from the general public, that haphazardness is continuously changing. Intellectual wisdom is god's blessing, and its duty is not to bully its subjects, vex them, or exploit them, but to serve them. Today people have lost their faith in the educated community. They think that they are more foreign than the foreigners. Is it a matter of surprise then that this community today is being battered from both sides? From the master's side because they think that except for their shelter they do not have any other, and by the public because they do not share any intimate relations with them. Their lifestyle, their speech, their attire, their thought and behaviour are different from the general public and this is only because we have become slaves of the English language. The situation is such that without the use of the English language nothing can work. But, now with the experience of so many days, it should be clear that if we cannot achieve our goal following this path, then why do we continue to stick to it? Just this previous year one inter-university commission sat to ponder over education-related issues. In it, one proposal was why should one's mother tongue not be the medium of education in place of English. The majority protested against this proposal, but why? It is because without an English medium, children would remain weak in English and will not be able to speak and write well in it. However, after all this devotion, over the past one hundred and fifty years, no Indian writer has written anything in English that could earn as much respect as a third grade English writer has in England. I don't remember whether it was Pandit Madan Mohan Malaviyaji, or it was Sir Tejbahadur Sapru,[76] who said, that even after fifty years of banging our heads, even today one takes time and hesitates to speak in English, thinking whether they have made a mistake or not! We ruin our eyes, hurt our backs and burn our blood to practise English, memorising their proverbs; but the compositions by even the greatest of Indian writers does not have any more merit than exercises done by school students. Just two to three days ago in Punjab, graduates who were being tested on their English proficiency were criticised by

76. Sir Tejbahadur Sapru (1875-1949) was a prominent Indian freedom fighter and politician who helped to draft the Constitution of India.

the examiners that the majority of students did not have the power to express their thoughts, in fact many made spelling mistakes. And this is the result after persevering on it for not less than twelve years. Even then, for us the medium of education in English is important—this is the view of our scholars. However, in Japan, China and Iran the medium of education is not English. Still, they are far ahead of us in every aspect of culture, but our boat will sink without the English medium. Our Marwari brothers are worthy of our thanks that at least as far as business is concerned, they have protected their community.

Friends, perhaps I have deviated from my topic, but my only hope is that we recognise how significant a task we have in front of us. We need to understand that the day we break the domination of English and create a common national language, it is on that day that we would witness *swarajya* or self-rule. I do not remember if any country has gained liberation on the strength of a foreign language. The basis of the nation is the national language. Nations are not made on rivers, mountains and seas. Language is that bond, which forever keeps the nation tied together and does not let it fall apart. The time when the British arrived, the feeling of nationalism had disappeared in India. It could be said that in them even a sense of political consciousness was not left. The British rule came and created a nation. If today the British were to depart—and this is bound to happen one or the other day—then where will our nation go? Is it not possible that each province turns into a state and then the same schisms arise? In the present state of our cultural consciousness, to keep alive and be cautious we need British rule to continue. If we want to come together as one nation to gain liberation, then we have to take the help of the national language and using that armour, we will have to construct our nation. Think about how crucial a work you are undertaking. You are not making lawyers who needlessly intervene in law, you are not creating workers for the state machinery, you are uniting a divided community, expanding the borders of friendship, and bringing long-forgotten brothers together. Considering how sacred this task is, there will be no hardship that one will not be able to welcome. This is not the path for seeking wealth, neither is it possibly the path for attaining glory, but there can be no better work than this for one's spiritual satisfaction. This is the value of your sacrifice. I am hopeful that this ideal will forever remain in front of you. You quite well understand the significance of this ideal. It dispels our hesitation giving us confidence, it banishes doubt and unease of our heart and it gives us the courage to face difficulties.

I would like to dwell briefly on our expectations from the national language. Whether you call it Hindi, Hindustani, or Urdu, it is the same thing. We do not have any arguments about the name. Whether we refer to God as *Ishwar* or *Khuda*, in our national language, both have an equal respect. If in our nation there are many people, who refer to *Ishwar* as 'God', then the national language will also welcome them. A living language keeps growing like a living body. The idea of pure Hindi is absurd. If India was inhabited only by Hindus then the national language could have been purely Hindi. Till such time as Muslims, Christians, Parsis, Afghanis, and other communities are present, our language will also remain all-encompassing. If Hindi wants to continue to be regional and wants to stay as a language exclusively for Hindus, then we can have a pure Hindi. It will have to be changed radically by changing its constituents. From full maturity it will again become a child; this proposition is impossible and laughable. Before one's eyes one has seen hundreds of foreign words entering language, and we could not stop them. To think that we can stop their attack is pointless. This will be a hindrance in the development of language. For trees to be strong and shapely it is given the support of a prop. Scholars can be monitored in such a way that inappropriate, distasteful or offensive words do not enter into usage, but this control can be established only on books. Any kind of control over conversational language is going to be difficult. But the minds of scholars are also strange. In Prayag, in a gathering of scholars and intellectuals in the 'Hindustani Academy,' there have been arguments over the words *'timahi,' 'sehmahi'* and *'traimasik,'*—all of which mean 'quarterly' in English—which has continued for several years now, but no decision has been taken yet. The protectors of Urdu are towards *'sehmahi'*, the protectors of Hindi are towards *'traimasik,'* poor *'timahi'* which is the simplest, easily spoken and understood word is being boycotted by both sides. The beauty of language can be protected by keeping its modesty locked up, but only at the cost of its life-likeness. Make its soul so strong, that it can protect both its modesty and health on its own. We will certainly have to keep such rustic words away, which are spoken in a particular area. Our ideal should be that our language is understood by more and more people. If we keep this ideal before us, then while writing as well, we will avoid getting trapped by clever words. It is misconstrued that incorporation of Persian words makes the language difficult. Such verses of pure Hindi can be given as examples whose meaning even scholars will find difficult to comprehend. Only those words are easy, which are used on a daily basis. There is no debate that it is Turkish, or Arabic, or Portuguese. I do not understand why there is such co-wifely relation of extreme jealousy between Hindi and Urdu. If people of one community love using the term 'Urdu,' then they should be allowed to use it. Those who love the term 'Hindi,' should be allowed to do so. Why should one fight over this? Needlessly fighting on seeing two names of the same thing and giving it so much importance that it becomes a hindrance in national unity is the mentality of a diseased and weak mind. From my experience, I can say, that for making Urdu our national language, our Muslim brothers are no less interested than our Hindus. I am interested in those Hindus and Muslims who are devoted to the cause of nationalism. I have nothing to do with conservatives. The camp of Urdu and Muslim culture today is Aligarh. There I spoke with professors of Urdu and Persian and those from other disciplines, and from them I gathered that they are as tired of the language of the maulvis, as with the language spoken by pandits, and they are earnestly ready to get involved in a Kaumi Bhasha Sangh Andolan (National Language Association Movement). I am prepared to accept that the Muslim community feels that staying away from Hindus would be beneficial—however the effectiveness of that faction is getting weaker every day—and if they want to stuff Arabic up their throats, then why should we fight them? Do you think that such a complicated language will be popular among the Muslim community? Never. Among the Muslims, only those writers are upheld who write in the language of the common people. The language of the maulvis does not stand a chance even here. I too have a certain right to request something to my Muslim friends because my life has been spent in the service of Urdu and even now I write as much in Urdu as in Hindi; belonging to the Kayastha caste, I have been practising Persian since childhood and Urdu comes more naturally to me than Hindi. My question is would you think of this as an attempt at strangulating the neck of Hindi? Do you know, and if not, then you should know, that the very first poet, who sowed the cultural seeds for Hindi (whose usage began long ago) was Amir Khusrau? Do you know that at least five hundred Muslim poets developed Hindi through their poetry, out of which many were top level poets? Do you know that even Akbar, Jahangir and Aurangzeb had an interest in Hindi poetry and that it was Aurangzeb who gave the name *rasna-vilas* and *sudha-ras*[77] for mangoes? Do you know that even today poets like Hasrat and Hafeez Jalandhari[78]sometimes write in chaste Hindi? Do you know that in Hindi there are thousands of words and verbs which have come from Arabic

77. *Rasna-vilas* and *sidha-vilas* are names given to two varieties of mangoes.
78. Abu Al-Asar Hafeez Jalandhari (1900-1982) was a Pakistani Urdu language poet who wrote the lyrics for Pakistan's National Anthem.

and Persian, and that they have been totally assimilated in it? If even after knowing this, you think of Hindi and Urdu as separate, then you are being unjust not only to your country but to yourself. When and where Urdu words began, for this there is no dated document available. Do you understand that phrases like *'vah bada kharaab aadmi hai'* (He is a very bad man) and *'vah bada durjan manushya hai'* (He is an extremely depraved human being) are two different languages? Hindus are comfortable with the word *'kharaab'* as well as *'aadmi'* but why are Muslims not at ease with words like *'durjan'* and *'manushya'*? In our national language, there is a place for both *durjan* and *sajjan* (gentleman), *umda* (good) and *kharaab*, till the point where its comprehensibility is not obstructed. Beyond this, we are neither friends of Urdu, nor of Hindi. The funny thing is that 'Hindi' is the name given by Muslims and till fifty years ago, what is now called Urdu used to be called Hindi by the Muslims. And today Hindi is scandalous. Can't you see that Hindi is a natural name? People from England speak English, people from France speak French, people from Germany speak German, people from the Persian community speak Persian, Turkish people speak Turkish, Arabs speak Arabic, then why should the people of Hind not speak Hindi? Urdu does not come in rhyme or repetition, in rhythm or stress. If Hindustan is called Urdustan, then the national language would definitely be Urdu. The worshippers of national language do not argue with names, they argue with reality. Why does not the vocabulary of the two languages become united? We need a common lexicon between the two languages, in which common words can be collected. In Hindi, to a certain extent my friend Pandit Ramnaresh Tripathi has fulfilled this need. This kind of lexicon should be there in Urdu too. Perhaps this work will be postponed till the Kaumi Bhasha Sangh (National Language Association) is created. I have this complaint about my Muslim friends that they avoid even common words in Hindi, although in Hindi common Persian words are used liberally.

But the question that arises is: to what extent can national language fulfil our needs? Novels, stories, travelogues, newspaper articles, criticism if it is not too cryptic: all this can be written in the national language if it is practised; but literature does not only comprise these. There are infinite branches of Philosophy and Science as well for which you cannot use the national language. Ordinary things can be written using simple words. In critical subjects, and novels as well, when it becomes psychological, you are compelled to take refuge in Sanskrit, Arabic and Persian words. If our national language is not complete in all respects, and if you cannot express every concern, every feeling in it, then this is a major flaw in it; and it is our duty to ensure that our national language is complete in all respects just like the prosperous languages of other nations. At present, both Hindi and Urdu in are not complete in themselves. Forget about being complete, they are not even incomplete. Those who have experience in writing in the national language, they will have to accept that for each expression they have to wrack their brains immensely. Easy words are not found, if found, then they are not used, they spoil the form of language just like a lump of salt spoils the taste of a sweet-dish like *kheer*.[79] The reason behind it is clear: that, knowledge of the language is very low among the masses and the number of common words is few. Until there is spread of education among people and their vocabulary does not expand, we cannot bring in meaningful criticism in a language they can understand. Our Hindi language itself is not older than a century, the national language is in infancy, and for the time being if we are able to write just simple literature, then we should be satisfied. Along with this, we should keep expanding the lexicon of national language. When the very words of Sanskrit and Arabic-Persian, which make us apprehensive, come into practice, the fear that we have of them will dissipate. The process action of language-

79. *Kheer* is an Indian dessert made of sweetened milk and rice or vermicelli.

development will only happen slowly. Along with this we will have to create a board of various regional language scholars, who are convinced of the usefulness of the national language. On that board, representatives of all languages including Urdu, Hindi, Bangla, Marathi, Tamil, etc., should be kept, and the responsibility of carrying out this process in an orderly manner and expediting it would be given to them. Till now we have run this movement spontaneously. We have not tried to seek help from others. Your Yatri Mandal has also been limited only to scholars of Hindi. There was no attempt to win the confidence of Muslim scholars from their centres of learning. Our scholars are overjoyed with their competence in English. Though they have been using public money to study Philosophy, Science and all other branches of knowledge prevailing in the world, they have continued to turn a blind eye to the people. Their world is different; they have inculcated a mentality of subservience. If only they had national consciousness, if only they had realised their duty towards the people, then our task would have been easier. How does it matter if some people flaunt their scholarship in English in a country where the percentage of education among people is so low? We would be convinced only when there is an attempt to improve the educational status of common people alongside intellectuals. It is not only English-speaking people who live in India. Out of a thousand, 999 people do not know the English alphabet. Is the world unjustified in not considering such a country as a nation whose people think and write in a foreign language? Till you have a national language, you do not have a nation. Both have a relationship of cause and action. You cannot fool the experts of politics, the British rulers, by claiming aloud to be a nation. They behave with you in such a manner knowing how hollow you are.

Now we have to think about how to expand the campaign for national language. It is with regret that I have to say that our leaders in this have shown criminal negligence. They are still under this illusion that this is a very insignificant issue, which will get done by insignificant people, and influential people like them do not have the time to get involved in the hassle. They have not understood the significance of this work until now; otherwise this would have been in the first line of their programme. In my view till the time there is such organisation, unity, harmony in the nation that people can communicate in one language, it will not even have the strength to attain independence. It is impossible. Those who are the leaders of the nation, those who stand in elections and win, with honest modesty I would request them that there will be hundreds of elections that will come and go, you will sometimes lose, sometimes win, but self-rule would be as far from you as heaven is. You might bring forth the core of your mind in English but because you do not have the backing of the nation, you will not even get the attention that a crying child does. When children cry, they are given sweets and toys. Those perhaps you will also get, so that your clamour does not interfere in your parents' work. Don't think of this work as insignificant. This is the foundation, and until your best slurry, mortar, cement and your ablest competency to build is not spent here, your building will not get constructed. You may build an earthen hut, which will get blown away with one strong breeze. Actually, what we have done till now is next to nothing. We have not been able to open a good school for national language. Every year several schools are opened, which are not required by the nation. Osmania University[80] is a worthwhile institution if it does not let the gulf between Hindi and Urdu widen. Still, I give it preference over other universities. There are quite a few educational institutions that promote servitude to English making students slaves of self-interests, needs, showmanship, and inaction, and what is laughable is that such training is transacted at a high price. The market value of this education is zero, then why are we

80. Osmania University, named after its founder Nawab Osman Ali Khan, the seventh Nizam of Hyderabad (now in the state of Telangana), was established in 1918.

pursuing it blindly like a herd of sheep? We do not acquire English education for attaining civility and refinement. Its objective is liberal. Before seeking refinement from the British, we need to realise that it is part of our heritage which has been deeply instilled in us. We will say that we are more civil than necessary. Our civility has pushed us to the limits of weakness. Whatever is there in Western civility is industry and courage. We did not pick those from it. What was selected was idleness, arrogance, selfishness, shamelessness, alcoholism and other bad habits. Go to an ignorant farmer; see how polite, hospitable, honest, and trustworthy he is. His corollary is Tommy, an English equivalent, embodying 'true' Western civility, by being a drunkard, a loafer, who is rowdy and impudent, and without shame. To learn refinement, we do not need to be slaves of the British. We should have such schools where the highest education can be attained with ease in the national language. At this moment one such school, if not more, should be there in a central place. But, even today, we continue to follow like herds the same system of schooling and education. Not one gentleman is born who might open one school of national language. Before my eyes scores of students from the Deccan went to Kashi to learn language, but there was no provision there. The same is the situation elsewhere. They returned after encountering several difficulties. Now there has been some provision for education of some students, but it is nothing, seeing the work that needs to be done. Staging good plays as a part of the campaign for promotion of Hindi may help us attain positive results. In this subject, our cinema is doing creditable work, although the kind of bad taste, dirt and squalor, the kind of sensual love and evil desires that are being spread through it diminishes the impact of this work. If we can stage good and thoughtful plays, it will definitely help in popularising the campaign. We need true missionaries and you have the responsibility of this mission. The great difficulty is that till the utility of an object is apparently visible, then why would anybody want to waste time on that? If our leaders and scholars were not ignorant of the significance of national language, if they could use the national language, then there would be a special attraction for it among the public. But here, we are intoxicated under the influence of Englishness. One more means of campaigning is to solicit the magazines in English and other languages of India that they mandatorily give one or two columns daily for the national language. If they accept our request, then it will be extremely beneficial. We are dreaming of that day when our national language will completely replace English; when our scholars will do their creative work in the national language; when the best works will emerge in the national language from Madras and Mysore, Dhaka and Pune, and all the other places; the best papers will be published in it. At the gatherings of languages and literatures of the world, Hindustani literature and language will acquire a proud place only when we refrain from participating in it either in borrowed frames or in our tattered ones, but in a manner befitting the stature of a world literature. Whether this dream will be realised or be subsumed in darkness would be decided by our sense of nationalism. If that seed has been sown in our heart, it will be sustained; but if it is only on the tip of our tongue, then it will dry up.

This is not the time to deliberate upon Hindi and Urdu literature, and even if we wanted to, we do not have the time. Our new literature has not completely developed in relation to other regional literatures. If all regional literatures can come into Hindi, then there is a possibility that it can be called complete. From Bengali, we have borrowed almost all its literary masterpieces, and from Gujarati and Marathi literature as well we have taken certain things. From Tamil, Telugu, and other languages, we have not been able to take anything, but we hope we can access this treasure, provided our confidantes help us. Our ancient literature is entirely poetic, and, though, there is ornamentation and devotion to a great degree, there is still plenty worthy of reading. If you have to read the creation of the Bhakti poets, then you should engage with Tulsi,[81] Sur,[82] and Mira,[83] when it comes to knowledge there is no match for Kabir,[84] and he is so excessive in ornamentation that he has almost outdone our ancient poetry. But it is not the fault of those poets, it is the fault of the circumstances in which those poets were compelled to live. In those days, art was patronised by the court and artists had to pander to the fancies of their benefactors. Even Urdu poets were in the same state. This was the general situation of those times. Our affluent sections were seekers of pleasure, and besides love, separation and detachment they could not think of anything else. Even if there is a trace of the living realities of life somewhere, then it is in this realisation that the world is transient, it is perishing, and that this world is a store of unhappiness, and the sooner one leaves it, the better it is. There seems to be nothing apart from this false asceticism. Yes, from the perspective of those who appreciate Urdu, it is considered invaluable that Urdu poetry still follows a similar course though its subject matter has attained a depth of some kind. In Hindi, the new has completely broken ties with the old. And today's Hindi poetry is marked by more depth, self-reflection, and portrayal of experiences compared to ancient poetry. The change of times has impacted it in such a way that today it is nothing but a cry of pessimism. The poet, however, does not get affected; in fact, his patience and sense of contentment is such that he is able to confront the biggest challenges and problems of the time. And because he expresses exactly those feelings which are intimate to all of us, his poetry has the capability to touch us. It is evident that not everybody has feelings and only a few

81. Tulsidas (1532-1623) was a Hindu Vaishnava saint and poet, also credited to be the author of the Indian epic Ramcharitamanas.
82. Surdas (dates uncertain) was a devotional poet and saint known for his lyrics written in praise of Krishna.
83. Mirabai (1498-1546) was a Hindu mystic poet of the Bhakti movement.
84. Kabir was a fifteenth century Indian mystic poet and saint who is said to have influenced the Bhakti movement.

of the poets express the sorrow of their hearts, many of them are governed by their imagination.

If you desire cultivation of sadness, then read the poetry of 'Mahadevi,[85]' 'Prasad,[86]' 'Pant,[87]' 'Subhadra,[88]' 'Lalli,' 'Divij,[89]' 'Milind,[90]' 'Naveen,[91]' Pandit Makhanlal Chaturvedi, etc. I have given the names of only those poets that I remember; there are several other poets like them, whose poetry will move you deeply. If you want to enjoy reading poetry, then read the works of Maithali Sharan Gupta[92] and Tripathiji. Tripathiji has presented the vast range and beauty of rustic literature. You may delve into it at will and see for yourself how uncommon, how sweet and poetic these village folk songs are. If you are interested in drama, then you should read the social and revolutionary plays of Lakshmi Narayan Mishra.[93] If your taste lies in historical and sentimental plays, then you may explore the works of 'Prasadji.[94]' In Urdu the best play that I came across has been written by 'Taj.[95]' It is '*Anarkali*.'

---

85. Mahadevi Verma (1907-1987) was a Hindi poet and educationist. She was one of the pioneers of the romantic movement in Hindi literature.
86. Jaishankar Prasad (1890-1937) was a well-known figure of modern Hindi literature.
87. Sumitranandan Pant (1900-1977) became the first poet of Hindi to receive the Jnanpith Award in 1968.
88. Subhadra Kumari Chauhan (1904-1948) was a Hindi poet best known for her poem 'Jhansi ki Rani.'
89. Janardan Prasad Jha 'Dwij' (1904-1964) was a Hindi poet and educationist.
90. Jagannath Prasad 'Milind' (1907-1986) was a Hindi poet and playwright.
91. Balakrishna Sharma Naveen (1897-1960) was a Hindi poet.
92. Maithili Sharan Gupt (1886-1964) was a Hindi writer considered to be a pioneer of poetry in Khari boli.
93. Lakshmi Narayan Mishra (1903-1987) was a popular Hindi playwright.
94. Jaishankar Prasad (1890-1937) was a famed figure in modern Hindi literature.
95. Syed Imtiaz Ali Taj (1900-1970) was an Urdu playwright.

If you are a devotee of the comic strain (*hasya rasa*), then read the creations of Annapurnanand.[96] If you want to witness the best representations of national language, then read the hilarious plays of G. P. Srivastava.[97] In the field of Urdu *hasya rasa* there are many top-quality writers and Pandit Ratannath Dar[98] has excelled in it. If you want to enjoy 'Umar Khayyam' in Hindi then immerse yourself in the '*Madhushala*' of the poet 'Bachchhan.[99]' You will find its fragrance enchanting. In fictional literature, you will find reflections of real life in the creations of 'Prasad,' 'Koushik,' 'Jainendra,[100]' 'Bhartiya,' 'Aggyai,[101]' and 'Visheshvar.' Among the Urdu novel writers, Sharar,[102] Mirza Ruswa,[103] Sajjad Hussain, Nazeer Ahmad,[104] etc., are famous, and in Urdu, the best writer in the national language is Khwaja Hasan Nizami,[105] who has the power to move us. In the field of Hindi novel writing, there have been few achievements so far but there have been indications of the emergence of new enthusiasm, new points of view, new messages which give us hope. We have no reason to be ashamed of the progress made in this era.

Friends, I have taken a lot of your time; however, one

96. Annapurnanand (1895-1962) was a writer known for his genteel humour.
97. Ganga Prasad Srivastava (1889-1976) was a Hindi writer known for his interest in comedy.
98. Ratan Nath Dar Sarshar (1846-1903) was an Urdu novelist and editor of the Lucknow newspaper Avadh Akbar.
99. Harivansh Rai Srivastava (1907-2003) was a Hindi poet of the 'Nayi Kavita' movement.
100. Jainendra Kumar (1905-1988) was a Hindi novelist.
101. Sachchidananda Vatsyayan (1911-1987) was one of the pioneers of the 'Nayi Kavita' Movement in Hindi literature.
102. Abdul Halim Sharar (1860-1926) was a prolific Urdu writer.
103. Mirza Hadi Ruswa (1857-1931) was an Urdu poet and writer of fiction, best known for his novel Umrao Jan Ada.
104. Nazeer Ahmad Dehlvi (1831-1912) was an Urdu writer and scholar.
105. Khwaja Hasan Nizami (1873-1955) was an Indian Sufi saint known for his essays written in Urdu.

issue of contention still remains, which I am hesitant to raise. I have been postponing it for so long but now a solution is necessary for that as well. That is the issue of a national script. Spoken language can be somehow brought together, but how can there be one script? In Hindi and Urdu script there is a difference as wide as the East and the West. For Muslims they feel as attached to their Persian script as Hindus love their Nagari script. Those Muslims who read as well as write Tamil, Bangla or Gujarati, they look at Urdu from a religious, devotional point of view; because the difference between Arabic and Persian scripts is the same as that between Nagari and Bengali scripts, in fact even less than that. For them, the Persian script is filled with whatever they hold dear—their pride in the ancient past, their cultural and historical heritage. In it there are certain shortcomings, but there are also some strengths, on whose basis they retain their relevance. It is shorthand of a kind. The first step to campaign for our national language and national script in a friendly way is to organise the Nagari script. If Bangla, Gujarati, Tamil, etc., accept the Nagari script, then to a large extent the question of national script would get resolved and, if nothing else, then the numbers themselves will help the Nagari script to attain supremacy. And learning of the Hindi script is so easy and through this script their writings and compositions will get such a popularity, that my prediction is they will easily accept it. We are not trying to eliminate the Urdu script. All we want is that we have a national script. If the whole nation adopts the Nagari script, then it is possible that Muslims will also accept the same. National consciousness will not allow them to stay away for too long. Wouldn't Muslims also not naturally desire that their magazines and books are read all over India? We do not want to erase any script. We only want that inter-regional interaction should happen in the Nagari script. Political awareness among Muslims will resolve this issue. In UP there is this movement going on as well that it be made mandatory in schools for Urdu students to have such knowledge of Hindi and for Hindi students to have such knowledge of Urdu that they can read minor books and write letters. We hope that such a movement becomes successful so that all students will become familiar with both the scripts, Hindi as well as Urdu. And when the language becomes one then Hindi because of its completeness will become all powerful and it will be used in different projects. Our job is precisely this that we awaken such a sense of national consciousness in people that they learn to willingly forego petty self-interests in the interest of the nation. You have taken responsibility for this task, and I know it was not on an impulse that you demonstrated such courage, but, that you have full faith in the mission, as you know that this faith, which is derived from truth and justice, strengthens the soul. In society there is always an abundance of such people who are involved in eating-drinking, accumulating money and engaging in life's other activities. This is the body of the society. Its life force comprises a few human beings, who always fight for their conservation—sometimes fight against blind faith, sometimes against ignorance, sometimes against disorder, and sometimes against subjugation. The foundation of society lies in the courage of such fighters. You are one of these soldiers. A soldier fights, without caring for victory or defeat. The only purpose he has is that he sacrifices himself for many others despite the several obstacles that confront him. It is possible that you will be ignored and neglected. People may also call you a freak or a lunatic. Let them say it. If your resolve is true, then each one of you will become a leading light. Your life should be such that people have faith and regard for you. You motivate others too with the fire of your zeal, as the victory of every idea depends on the living example of its proponent. The highest objective can become reprehensible in the hands of incompetent people. I have faith that you will not let yourself become incompetent.

[Speech/article. Published in *Hans*, January 1935 (speech delivered on the occasion of the fourth Convocation and degree distribution ceremony of the Dakshin Bharat Hindi

Prachar Sabha, on 29 December 1934). Compiled in 'Sahitya ka Uddesh' and 'Kuchh Vichar.']

Translated by Sango Bidani

29. Our Hindi Prachar Yatra in South India (*Dakshin Bharat mein Hamari Hindi Prachar Yatra*)

The Dakshin Bharat Hindi Prachar Sabha (Council for Promoting Hindi in South India) was kind enough to have given us the opportunity to meet those devoted to Hindi and to see for ourselves the success of their campaign there. This year, the Council invited me to deliver the keynote speech on the occasion of the convocation ceremony; I left Bombay on December 27 and reached Madras on December 28. I was accompanied by the owner of the Hindi Granth Ratnakar Karyalaya (Hindi Publishing Company), Shri Nathuramji Premi,[106] and the leading activist of the Hindi Prachar Sabha, Bombay Unit, Shri R. Sankaran. We travelled by third class; yet we did not suffer any remarkable discomfort on our way. Premiji had carried *magdal laddoos*[107] and *pooris*[108] with him. Ever since Premiji has been ill, he is extremely cautious in matters of eating and drinking. On our way, we ate many *laddoos*. There are a very few railway stations in these parts where *puris* are available, and where they are found, they are rather awful. At one station, we ate *idlis* for the first time. *Idlis* are made of rice and skinned black lentil flour. In equal quantities, the two flours are mixed and kneaded together, and the dough is allowed to stay overnight which makes it slightly sour. The next day, the dough is made into thick cakes and steamed. Eating *idlis* is quite the custom in this region. If you look around in a hotel, you see everyone eating only *idlis*,

---

106. Shri Nathuram Premi (1881-1960) was a Hindi writer and poet.
107. *Magdal laddoos* are traditional balls of sweets made from roasted green gram lentils, ghee (clarified butter), sugar and dried whole milk, popular in the northern part of the Indian subcontinent.
108. *Puris* are unleavened deep fried breads made of whole wheat or refined flour in the Indian sub-continent.

dal, and *chutney*. Here nobody loves sweets. But yes, because of the intimacy of interaction with north India, sweets have become more popular.

In Madras, we were hosted by Ramnathji Goenka.[109] Fortunately, Shri Kaka Kalelkarji[110] also happened to be staying there, and we had the pleasure of seeing him. He is service incarnate and his constructive contribution to the spread of Hindi is hopeful and promising. Unless the utility of something is not obviously seen, our love for it does not endure. How to make the knowledge of Hindi useful is the only question that comes before him. All big businesses are in the hands of the British; Hindi cannot have its way there. However in the small businesses, which are in the hands of Indians, there might be some benefit if Hindi is brought into use. He is studying the situation for exactly this purpose. Our best wishes are with him. Goenkaji is among those men of fortune who not only know how to earn money but also to put it to good use. His generosity is the source of financial help to many public institutions—as far as the spread of Hindi is concerned, in this endeavour, he stands tall and firm like a pillar. He remains absolutely untouched by arrogance. He is a jovial, guileless, and industrious young man, and fittingly the Treasurer of the Council. We stayed at his house for five days and it was as good as being in one's own home.

The convocation was held at the Gokhale Hall. I expected a huge gathering, but I learnt that the Hindi-lovers had gone out of the city on account of vacation. The railways had arranged to dispatch many people out of Madras by selling cheap tickets. Though the spectators were few, everyone present had some connection with the spread of Hindi, and seeing the missionary zeal of the campaigners, our minds were filled with hope and pride. There were people who had travelled

109. Shri Ramnath Goenka (1904-1991) launched the Indian Express in 1932.

110. Kaka Kalelkarji (1885-1981) was a journalist and an activist during the Indian Independence Movement.

hundreds of miles, and there were among them a great number of women. More than cultural, the founding principle of this movement is political, which aspires to see the entire nation unified through a single national language. So, it has drawn the support of eminent leaders of this province as well as those of the most sacrificing supporters. It is not surprising that this Council, which is led by Shri Rajgopalacharya as its Director and Shri K. Nageshwar Rao as its Vice-President—who hold office not only in name but take interest in every activity of the organisation—is becoming popular and influential quite rapidly. There was a total of seventeen hundred takers of the examination at the Prathmik (elementary), Madhyama (middle), and Rashtrabhasha (national) levels in 1930, the number rose to nine thousand and sixty in 1933; and it dwindled to four thousand one hundred and forty one in 1934. This makes one suspect that the findness for Hindi may be waning. If it is so, it would be a cause for distress. It is our duty to work towards investigating the causes of this decline and attempt to deal with them.

There are only two places worth seeing in Madras—one is the seven-mile long coastline and the other is Adyar, the Headquarters of the Theosophical Society[111]. A coastline as beautiful as this is not to be found anywhere else. One can walk for miles along the coast and enjoy the cool breeze. Adyar is a kind of colony, eight miles from the coast. Its area must not be less than two square miles. It is a very well maintained, clean place, lined with plants. It has a library, printing press, temple, canteen, and lodges for employees and other theosophists. In the centre there is an enormous, age-old banyan tree, under the shade of which a gathering of as many as almost two thousand people can be accommodated. They say it was under this tree that the late Mrs. Annie Besant would sit sometimes and deliver sermons to quench the thirst of seekers of faith. This *tapobhoomi*, sacred place for meditation, is a joy to behold. These days, the annual festival of the Theosophical Society

111. The Theosphical Society in Adyar was established in 1882.

is being celebrated and it has drawn representatives of the Society from across the globe.

At two gatherings, I had the opportunity to speak to the chief campaigners of the province. Three of the men are from North India, and have made South India their home. These worthy gentlemen seemed to have heart-felt devotion to the cause of campaigning for Hindi. We saw enthusiasm in all of them. They perform this work with passion, and not merely as an occupation. They love literature and they were found to be ever eager to listen to and participate in discussions on literary topics. Shri Devdootji Vidyarthi, who is the leader of the Hindi Prachar Sabha in the province of Kerala and a resident of the province of Bihar, has published two anthologies of prose-poetry and is also writing a play. On reading these collections, one knows how delicate his feelings are and how thorough his imagination is. Along with that, he has a total command over the language too.

One evening, we got the opportunity to witness the theatrical talents of the campaigners. For two years now, a few people got together to form a theatre academy (*natak parishad*) and to promote it, they performed a play or two each year. The group has not had any performances this year due to some differences. It is my appeal to all those men to keep the objective of the group in mind, forget their individual differences of opinion and not let this part of the campaign fall weak. The two-three scenes that I had seen from the play *Durgadas* makes me reach the conclusion that with some restraint, the actors here can be very successful. In one scene, they had enacted the role of Chanakya. I liked this part very much. The dialogues of Chanakya were ridden with pain, hurt and defiance—a defiance which challenges even the existence of God; a defiance which looks at the world as the *rangasthal* or stage for deceit, pretence, injustice, and oppression.

Madras has two museums. One meant for animals and birds, while the other was for aquatic animals. The zoo is quite ordinary but the aquarium is extremely beautiful. Such a unique, variegated, and wonderful collection of fishes is not to be found anywhere else in the country (Bharatvarsha). Glass cases filled with water, within which fishes of different hues and colours played, is an extremely charming sight.

The Sabha has rented two apartments. In one, there is their office, library, examination division, etcetera and, in the other, is the press. For both, a rent of Rs. 350 is given. Mantriji (Secretary) is on the lookout for a house where both the jobs can go on. If a place like that is found, then perhaps there could be some saving on the rent and the work could be carried out in a more organised way. It is not a matter of pride for Hindi lovers that a rent of rupees three and a half thousand has to be paid annually by an organisation as useful as this, since it does not have its own building. The reason for this appears to be that we still have not understood the significance of the campaign for Hindi. The onus of this lies much more on north India than the south.

Hindi, or Hindustani, is like a foreign language in South India. Most of the teachers are also people from the south. For students, besides reading textbooks, there would be little chance of practising Hindi. A consequence of this could be that their knowledge of the language would remain bookish. Some instances of this were also found. We met a number of gentlemen who could read Hindi from the textbook but could not speak it nor could they understand a lecture or speech in Hindi comfortably. If teachers in the classrooms speak to the pupils only in Hindustani and take care that students too use Hindustani, at least in the classrooms, then they would acquire the habit of speaking it chastely and they would then not make such comical errors; some specimens of which were narrated by a witty campaigner and that made us laugh heartily. A second appeal I wish to make to the campaigners of Hindi is that they must read Hindi pamphlets and newspapers so that they expand their knowledge of the language. Those who are fond of creative writing must keep writing in the papers and periodicals. There must be several things in the literature of the South, which when brought to Hindi, would fortify the cultural unity of the North and the South.

From Madras, on the fifth day we proceeded to Mysore. A narrow gauge train goes to Mysore. The train was extremely crowded, but we managed to sit. The chief campaigner in Mysore, Shri Hiranmayji, was our guide. Shri Jambunathji from Bangalore was also in the same compartment. In front of me sat a gentleman from Kerala. We spoke at length about literature and the Hindi language campaign. Though he was attached to the campaign, he also harboured the fear that the campaign might lose steam. It is natural to have a fear such as that. Our campaigns begin with such fervour, but within a few days people grow indifferent to the cause, that in spite of seeing a campaign alive, we cannot get rid of our doubts. I reassured my companion that the campaign was no longer merely run by one or two odd enthusiasts, it had grown to become an organisation with a strong foothold amidst the general public—with the hope that it will expand successfully. We reached Mysore in the morning. The Hindi-lovers there welcomed us and we stayed at Krishna Bhavan. Here we had everything we needed and the generosity which Shri Shivprasadji, the owner of the hotel, showed in his hospitality cannot be adequately praised. He must not be more than 28-30 years. His childhood was ridden with difficulties, to such an extent that he had to run away from home at the age of twelve and came away to Bangalore becoming a help at a hotel. With the experience he gained there and the assistance of his friends, he gathered the means and strength to establish this hotel. The consequence of his hard work is the independence he enjoys now. He shows special interest in literature and religion; he has liberal opinions, there is no trace of any religious orthodoxy. Along with intellectual progress and commercial growth, he has taken care of his physical improvement too. He practises Surya-Namaskar[112] and exercises regularly.

112. Surya-Namaskar, a series of yoga asanas, that is, yogic postures, is paying devotion to the Sun God.

Unlike ordinary *vaishyas* (traders), he does not find fulfillment in merely accumulating wealth. He has also acquired physical strength. He is a physically fit and healthy young man, and does not let any ill habits hover around him. In the worst of times, what all can an industrious man achieve? This is the lesson that can be derived from Shri Shivprasadji's life. I felt pleased to see that he had not let money become his master but had made it serve him. The objective of his life is to be of service to others. His desire is to establish a good gymnasium in his hometown Bulandsheher so that the youth will have a chance to strengthen its health and physical fitness. How virtuous a goal it is!

Adjacent to Krishna Bhavan is another hotel called Anand Bhavan. The owner there is Badriprasadji. This is the first hotel by North Indians in Mysore. And it is being run in a very organised manner. Badriprasad Ji has a very favourable disposition; he is eager to be of service and is a man who enjoys literature. He is also well acquainted with the developments in Hindi literature. He is a resident of Bulandsheher too but stays here in Mysore with his family. He took the responsibility of taking us to the chief tourist sights around Mysore and we are grateful to him for it.

Although there are many things to see in Mysore, but we didnot have time, so we had to satisfy ourselves with seeing only those places which are connected to Mysore and which would require the least amount of time to look around. Mysore is a clean, pleasing city, adorned with beautiful gardens. Wherever you go, there is a park, so much so that you see columns of flowers even along the railway tracks. The roads are wide, free of dust and dirt, with squares adorned with flowers and greens at every junction. There is such abundance of electricity here, that there is light even in the villages—and it is also extremely cheap. It costs only two *anas*[113] per unit in the villages. In other cities, only municipalities have light. Outside those, there is only darkness. Here, every pucca road

113. One ana is 1/16th of a rupee.

has electric light—and if you look at the town from Chamunda hilltop, it would seem that electric lights have spread a net over it. The hill is close to the town and is often visited by people, in the morning and evening, who go there for fresh air. It must be about a thousand feet high. There is a motorable road to reach the top. On it, there are electric lights. The Chamunda Devi temple is situated at the peak. A beautiful bungalow has been built higher up for the King's lodging. Chamunda Devi is the family goddess of the King of Mysore and the King often comes here to pray.

The old capital of Mysore, Seringapattam, lies at a distance of ten to twelve miles from Mysore Nagar. A motorable road has reached here. Seringapattam once used to be a bustling settlement, however now more and more people have left it to settle down in other towns and cities. The Purana Qila (Old Fort) is all but destroyed. The boundary wall stands in some places. The most beautiful sights here are the mausoleums of Hyder Ali and Tipu. In the centre of a delightful garden stands the impressive structure of the mausoleum made of black stone. There is some extremely beautiful inlay work inside the building while the doors display ivory work, which is the unique art of Mysore. Right outside the fort is Tipu Sultan's palace called Daria Daulat Bagh. Tipu Sultan used to rest here during summer. The exterior walls of the palace depict almost all the scenes of historical and political events of those times—these are quite similar to those that artists of the city depict even today on the walls; however the mosaic inside is very intricate. The place where the Sultan used to meet his subjects, that durbar is not any less grand than the Durbar-e-Aam in Delhi.

We went to see Krishna Raja Sagar (lake) from Seringapattam. It is a huge lake, fashioned out of blocking the River Cauvery by a dam. The dam is approximately two miles long and approximately 150 feet high. It is wide enough to allow motor-cars to ply up and down easily. In constructing the dam, the Mysore government has spent more than two crore rupees (20 million). A canal has been extracted out of this lake which irrigates nearly fifty miles of the surrounding area. A consequence of this is that with effort paddy and sugarcane have begun to grow here. To use the sugarcane, a sugar mill has also been constructed by the government. This water is also used for production of electricity. Altogether, this has cost the estate almost five crore rupees. There is no bigger dam than this in India. Beneath the dam is a pleasant place known as Vrindavan. One can see a unique play of fountains here. Water from the river has been drained down a slope with great force. On both sides is the splendour of the fountains, alongside which, electric bulbs are lit inside colourful glass coverings. When the reflection of the coloured light falls on the prancing water, it appears as if coloured water is emanating out of the fountains. From afar, the rainbow-like view bewitches the eye.

The palace of Mysore is also worth seeing, though there is nothing remarkable in this. The palaces, even of kingdoms whose subjects suffer hellish ordeals, manage to bewitch the eye. Amongst our kings, ninety-nine per cent of them siphon off a large part of the estate's revenue for their own gratification enjoyment and pleasure. The subjects of such kingdoms exist purely so that they can earn and earn for their Raja Sahib (his royal highness) to squander, and nothing must escape their lips, lest their tongues be cut off. Mysore is a wealthy kingdom, and the palace must complement its grandeur. One can keep admiring the décor of each of the halls. The pomp and grandeur of the Durbar Hall is unmatched in any of the states. During the occasion of Dussehra, the King occupies the throne while his ministers and workers take their chairs according to their ranks. He is welcomed with the customary *itr* (perfume) and *paan* (betel leaf), however the Indra[114] of this Indrapuri, despite being the lord of unparalleled glory, is a devotee of the virtue of sacrifice. Unlike other *riyasats* or estates, the durbar here is not a wrestling ground of Lord

114. The King of the Devas (Gods) in the Hindu pantheon.

Indra, but a hermit's *ashram*. The King receives twenty-two lakh rupees from the kingdom annually, but this sum is used for the betterment of the people, not for the wanton pleasures of the ruler. This is the reason why the people here worship their king and are proud of him. The King is fond of music and exercise, and has an interest in literature too.

After seeing the Mysore zoo, when one sees the zoological parks of Bombay and Madras, one feels as one does on being taken to a shanty after having visited a palace. The unique variety of birds, animals, and aquatic creatures found in Mysore, can probably be found nowhere else, except in the zoos of Calcutta. An establishment, such as this, of natural surroundings for animals can hardly be found anywhere else. All the creatures that we saw looked well-nourished, clean, and joyful.

The government has established a silk factory in Mysore, as well as a factory for sandalwood oil. This estate, which has been leased out, has a monopoly over sandalwood. Its business is in the hands of the government. They also have a skill development centre, where they impart education on wood, cane, ivory, paddy cultivation, pottery, and so on. The items crafted here are both exhibited and sold, however the rates are exorbitant. The most commendable thing we learnt here is that there is no terror of either the state's workers or the police, and there is little mention of bribery. In my opinion, there couldn't be a greater proof of a state's efficiency.

I witnessed a feeling of pure unity among the activists and leaders for the campaign of Hindi in Mysore. All the men have missionary zeal and affection towards Hindi. Pandit Hiranyamayji is a quiet worker, who perhaps envisions the campaign even in his dreams. Shri T. Krishnamoorthy and Shri K. Srinivasmoorthy, are both the secretaries of the campaign here, and not mere holders of office, but those who administer the Sabha and bring life to it. Both the men are teachers in the education department, but have adopted the campaign as their very own passion. Another enthusiast of the campaign is Mr. J. P. Verma. He works with the Inter University Board; he must have stayed here only for a year, but he shows such zeal in his support towards the campaign for Hindi that it is infectious. Given his enthusiasm, he does not care for the hurdles before him. He has a desire to create a circle for the welfare of 'Hindustani' by organising the North Indians living here. Irrespective of whether there is a response to it or not, he continues his narrative. Finally, he managed to have the circle inaugurated by me; though I carried out the ceremony of laying the foundation stone, the onus of raising a building there falls on those men who not only want to make money through business but also want to devote a portion of it to their compatriots. In fact, the responsibility also falls specifically on those who see and take stock of the world's progress.

My mind was filled with happiness on meeting Indira *behen* (sister) in Mysore. I had met this lady in Kashi, Prayag, and Delhi. She has spent two years at the Prayag Mahila Vidyapeeth acquiring special knowledge of Hindi and now she is campaigning for it here. She is the wife of Shri Krishnamoorthy Ji, the secretary of the campaign's committee. Her love for Hindi drew her to Prayag. Her husband also happily gave her the permission. She left her little daughter at home and went to Prayag. Why won't a movement be successful when it has such devotees? The other lady is Shrimati Laxmi Amma.[115] At this advanced age, she has passed 'Visharad'[116] and is now learning Urdu. Her enthusiasm is indefatigable, it puts youngsters to shame. She was always there to welcome me wherever I went. We went to her cottage with the veneration one has when one visits a temple; there we spent five to ten minutes, and it was as if one had met one's long-lost sister; she, in those few minutes tried fulfilling all her desires for showering us with affection

115. Amma means mother, it is often also used as a familiar form of address.
116. Prathama, Madhyama, Visharad, Sahitya-Ratna: four levels of examination in Hindi.

and hospitality. We were fortunate to have also met Professor Sustri. He is a teacher of Persian at the University of Mysore and knows Urdu well. He is fond of Hindustani and is an expert of the Sanskrit language. These days, he is translating the *Bhagavad Gita* into Persian. If the valuable thoughts on the Hindu-Muslim issue that he has expressed were to be adopted by our leaders, India today would be like paradise. He is living like an ascetic. Communal temperament is something that he loathes. The spiritual calm I earned sitting at his feet can be achieved only through divine vision. We also had the good fortune of meeting and interacting with one more supporter of Hindi, Professor Nanjun Daiya. He is the Professor of English at Mysore University. He is unwell these days. The generosity with which he welcomed us would continue to be a very sweet impression throughout our lives. He is studying Urdu these days, and many of my Urdu works have been read by him. Seeing his unsoiled love for literature and his ever-increasing respect for a small writer like me makes me contented. My only complaint against him is that his present of a cigarette case carved out of ivory has taught me that smoking may be a good habit—and since then my love for cigarettes has grown. I cannot see the box empty—for if there is no ink in the inkpot it is as good as an earthen pot—and when the box filled with cigarettes lies in front of me, then resisting the temptation is difficult.

Though I was given the opportunity to express my opinions about Hindi at two gatherings, it was a special treat to have got the chance to meet the soldiers of the Hindi language at the university. They were no less than fifty in number, and they were all young, studying at the university. But, they love Hindi so much that they always offer something or the other to the campaign. These men are the enthusiastic supporters of the language, and the credit for its popularity must go to them. Many of them read out self-composed poetry and prose, and we sat with our cups of coffee, chatting over literary conundrums for nearly an hour.

The state-language of Mysore is Kannada and there are about one crore and fifty lakh speakers of the language; however these speakers are spread across Madras, Bombay, Hyderabad State, and Mysore, and that has brought hurdles to the growth of the language. Ancient literature in Kannada is of supreme quality and new literature is also making steady progress. Bangalore has an office for the Kannada literary academy, a library, and this has led to the publishing of some of the best Kannada literature. I got the opportunity to be present in the service of many Kannada literary worshippers in Mysore. Like other languages of the provinces, Kannadiga (speakers of Kannada language) have also begun to worry if the campaign for Hindi will affect the growth of Kannada. It seems that the emergence of such a doubt lies in the misconception of the objective of the campaign of Hindi. The campaign for Hindustani assuredly does not intend to usurp the place of the provincial languages; it intends to occupy that spot which English has reserved for itself in India. The relationship between the national and regional languages will be just as the relationship between the provincial councils and the Indian assembly. The assembly does not interfere in any of the affairs of the provincial councils. Yes, there are some concerns that pertain to the entire country, and the assembly mediates those affairs. Our aim is to have Hindi, instead of English, as the medium of communication each time a writer or reporter promotes his/her book or pamphlet throughout the country. After all, a day will come, even if in the distant future, when India would sit alongside other nations upholding her culture and literature. If we consider India not a country but a continent with several countries within it, then also we would require a chief language to carry out internal transactions. It would be different if the countries maintained no relations with each other at all. In that situation, not even one province would be able to sustain its power. In my opinion, the campaign for Hindustani opens up a great space for fame and success for worshippers of literature, however there should be absolutely no reason for regional languages to become suspicious of it all. All that we have done till now has been done accommodating the perspective of the regional languages. If we create a repository containing technical terms and another one, a general lexicon, both are to be made separately. If we had had an inter-province council or a national language council which brought together experts of each of our languages over a few days or over a few weeks every year to deliberate over the concerns related to the national language, we might have accomplished the goal of a robust national language within ten to twenty years. Lack of coordinated efforts causes misutilisation of time and energy. Many terms used in philosophy, science, and religion are known by many names, however they could be known by the same words in all the regional languages. It would prevent the wracking of brains individually.

We left for Bangalore after five days of enjoying hospitality in Mysore. Bangalore to Mysore is a four-hour long journey. The views on the way are extremely pleasing. Some places have green farms, some others have mango, coconut, areca nut orchards and then in some places are tall mountains covered in greenery. Clouds dotted the sky and in the mellow light, the mountains could be seen. The beauty of the place had a dream-like quality. One could see villages nestled between the laps of the valleys, the white-washed walls of the huts communicated the cleanliness and good taste with which the villagers would have set up the village. The soil is red here because of which the farms look even more beautiful. The attire of the farmers seen working in the field was *kurta* and *janghiya* (shorts). Compared to a dhoti, the *janghiya* is a thing of frugality. Fields of paddy were also found in plenty, all of which were irrigated through canals. Now they also grow sugarcane here; and the state has set up a sugar mill.

We reached Bangalore in the evening. Shri Nittar, President of the Prachar Sabha, Shri Niwas Rao, Shri Jambunathan Ji, and a few others were present at the station. We were hosted by the President.

Bangalore is situated at a height of 3000 metres above sea level and is somewhat cooler than Mysore. The city is divided into two sections. One part comes under the administration of the Kingdom of Mysore, while the cantonment is governed by the British. The population is more than three lakh people approximately. There is nothing special about the city, it is comparable to Prayag or Lucknow, however the cleanliness of the cantonment roads and the ornamentation of the bungalows charms the mind. In Bangalore and in most of the South, houses don't have courtyards. Based on status, the houses have two to four small rooms. A small front lawn and a boundary wall are also constructed in front of the house. Every house looks like a bungalow.

The first day, early in the morning, we went to Lal Bagh for a walk. Its area is about a hundred acres. The structure, cleanliness, and beauty of the place, the tidy paths, the flower beds, and glass pavilion charm the heart. Interestingly, the park memorializes the good taste and love of trees that Sultan Hyder Ali had. They sell potted plants and seeds, and a variety of plants brought from outside India are grown here. The most attractive site in Bangalore is this park.

Only three miles from Bangalore stands the renowned institute which was founded by Shri Jamshedji Nusserwanji Tata.[117] To come to Bangalore and not see this would be unfortunate. We reached there around three in the afternoon on Sunday. The institute was closed but we were welcomed warmly by Dr. (Sir) C.V. Raman[118] and he also showed us the department of chemistry, the library, and the laboratories. I have met a couple of scientists earlier too. They are indeed well-coordinated, alluring, mysterious, humourless and self-contented. For scientists, contemplating nature's infinite

117. Shri Jamshedji Nusserwanji Tata (1839-1904) was the Indian industrial who established the Tata group of industries.
118. Sir C.V. Raman (1888-1970) was an Indian physicist who won the Nobel Prize in Physics in 1930.

mysterious creations perhaps reduces human beings to mere animals too, however, I was astonished to meet this prince of scientists. I have not ever seen a man so jovial, every inch of whose body bustles with the easy buoyancy of a child. He is a lover of science. This love for science is manifest in his eyes, his expressions, and his entire being. Running from one place to the other, he showed us each of the objects, like a child excited and impatient to show his intimate friend all his playthings and clothes, and wanting to show all his possessions at once, leaving nothing out. If I may say that his heart rests in this institute, it would not be wrong. Each and every corner, each and every flower and each and every plant, even to the extent that the charming natural view fills him with pride—almost as if this natural splendour was also his creation. It is only a scientist who would know how much this institute has benefited the country till now. We came back with the personality of Sir Raman stamped in our hearts. As the electrical department and other departments were closed, we could not see them. Sir Raman showed us an amusing spectacle—which was a mere sport for us, but for the learned, it was a matter of substantive research. If on the leather surface of the *tabla*,[119] a pinch of sand is sprinkled, and given a pat, the sand at times would take the form of a straight line, and at times become circular. The distinct individual beats of the *tabla* make themselves appear in a variety of patterns. Which dead soul would not be invigorated to see Sir Raman sprinkle the sand and pat the *tabla* with such liveliness and zest.

We left Doctor sahab at four in the afternoon thinking that if great people, instead of making monuments of their greatness, could turn it into a flame, then it would lighten up the world.

That day itself we saw the ceramic-utensil factory, which was adjacent to the institute. Their technique is quite similar to that of the traditional potter's. There is a special kind of clay that comes out from here in which, one or two things

119. An Indian percussion instrument consisting of a pair of drums.

when mixed prepares a paste. The paste is poured into different moulds and then taken out, subsequently, it is dried, coloured, and heated in the furnace. In the showrooms, there is a good collection of toys, figurines, and vases which tells us the progress that has been made in this field of work. Pipes, tiles, marble, toys made of wires—all these things are manufactured here. In the princely state of Mysore, there is a lot of use of electricity; all ceramic items that are required for it are manufactured in the factory itself.

Just like in Mysore, in Bangalore too the campaign for Hindi is going well. The National High School here has made Hindi a compulsory subject. Some vocational courses are also taught. There was a conference here in which the President was Professor A.R. Wadia. Professor Wadia is the President of the Hindi Prachar Sabha in Mysore. We were not able to meet him in Mysore, but we got that opportunity here. He has a special liking for Hindi and Urdu though he speaks in English, and that too, very well. The school Headmaster, Shri Sampatrao Giri (MA), is also devoted to Hindi and he has translated Tulsidas' *Ramayana* in prose-form in Kannada. Adjacent to the school is a gymnasium, which was inaugurated by Mahatmaji the previous year.

There are quite a few organisations managed by women in Bangalore, and Hindi is taught in almost all of them. Stitching, knitting, spinning, cane-work, music, embroidery are run in almost all the organisations. Teaching and management are expressly in the hands of women. At some places, there are gymnasiums for girls too. This awakening of women signals a hopeful future for the nation. The temperate climate here seems quite favourable for the pursuit of music. Music is popular among women. *Veena*[120] is a popular instrument here. If twice a month, these women could visit the neighbourhood villages, then, the women there would receive some light of their

---

120. A stringed instrument in Indian classical music. It is the instrument seen in the hands of Saraswati, the goddess of knowledge and culture.

awakening. Though all the organisations are progressing, but the development of Malleshwaram Mahila Samaj (Women's Society in Malleshwaram) is particularly noteworthy. It was in 1930 that Hindi classes were held here. There were only four women who appeared for the exam in the first year; and in the previous year, the number increased to forty-five. Two women from this organisation are studying in Prayag Mahila Vidyapeeth (Women's School in Prayag). Till now three hundred women from this society have acquired a working knowledge of Hindi. Here there is a society for improving spoken skills as well, in which women debate and discuss social issues. Not only this, a Hindi tri-monthly magazine named *Samaj Bharti* is taken out from here in which women write on different subjects. From time to time, lectures by scholars and national leaders are also held here. Once, Mahatmaji too had come here to deliver a lecture. Which organisation would not be proud of such glorious work?

The Kannada Bhasha and Sahitya Parishad (Kannada Language and Literature Council) is also there in Bangalore. With great respect and devotion, we did a *parikrama* (circumambulation) of this literary temple. The Parishad has a huge building of its own, in which there is one hall, one library, one reading room, and an office. Several notable works in Kannada have been published by the Parishad. These days, with positive encouragement from the King of Mysore, the Parishad is compiling a comprehensive dictionary of Kannada-English, whose editor and director of the editorial board is an elderly man named Professor Venkat Narayanappa. The zeal and diligence he shows in his work would put young people to shame. He was previously a teacher of chemistry at Mysore University. Now, he receives pension. Kannada literature has ancient roots and poetry in Kannada is especially remarkable. New literature is also being produced at a great pace. We also got to meet the respected Vice-Chairman Shri Gundappaji. He is a celebrated writer and poet, and a great scholar of ancient literature. The magnificence of Kannada literature is proven by the fact that towards the close of the twentieth century, there were nearly twelve hundred Kannada poets, of which twenty-five were women and another twenty-five were the King and other wealthy men. A scholar has bound their life-sketches in three volumes, thus setting the foundation for the history of Kannada literature. If certain elements from Kannada literature could come into Hindi, then this exchange would be advantageous to both the languages. Kumar Vyas's immortal composition *Bharat* is most likely the best piece of Kannada literature. Scholars of Kannada literature claim that a poet such as that is a rarity. Now that this region is witnessing campaigning for Hindi, perhaps there would be renditions of gems of Kannada literature into Hindi. *Hans* carries commentary on thought-provoking writings from Gujarati, Marathi, Urdu, and English magazines. If a Hindi-knowing Kannada scholar were to write comments on contemporary Kannada literature and send the commentary to *Hans,* the magazine will not only graciously accept it but treat it as a matter of pride.

The *vyayam-mandir,*[121] or gymnasium, by Mr. K. B. Iyer in Bangalore is also worth a visit. I wonder why Mr. Iyer decided to call it the Hercules Gymnasium; after all, our very own Hanuman Ji is no less than Hercules. If Hercules broke a mountain into two, Hanuman Ji swallowed the sun and carried the Dhaulagiri mountain on his palm for twenty-five hundred miles. Training for all types of exercises takes place here. Iyer himself is a man with impressive physique, and a few of his trainees are quite like body-builders. He has innovated an exercise regime based on the Surya-namaskar and has published literature on it. We could not meet him as he was out the day we visited. From the illustrated booklets that we read, we inferred that he had brought together modern and traditional methods to come up with a scientific practice routine which shows astounding results within a short span

121. Vyayam Mandir technically means an institution that provides physical education and training.

of time—to think that this *pahalvan*[122] used to be skinny in his childhood! We need more such gymnasiums in each city, in fact, I am sure people will welcome such an initiative.

Hindi in Mysore is still an optional subject. A movement to make Hindi a compulsory subject has started among the campaigners of Hindi. If this movement becomes successful, the campaign for Hindi will grow at twice the rate. With the intention to have a conversation regarding the same, I called upon the Diwan of Mysore State, Mirza Ismail.[123] Diwan sahab is a generous man, and has an interest in promoting education. We conversed in Hindustani. He is quite well acquainted with literature in Urdu, and speaks the language unhindered. He was also of the opinion that Hindustan is in need of a national language. Though he is sympathetic to the cause of the campaign, he is not in favour of taking administrative measures on a cultural issue. Until the campaign gains enough momentum to have a majority in the Executive Committee in favour, the state does not think it fit to intervene. It all depends on the campaigners' patience, exuberance, and service. Until Hindustani is accepted as the national language by consensus, how will the state accept it? Diwan sahab was thoroughly cordial with me. The whites have taught us that genteelness and entitlement do not mingle well. Diwan sahab is an exception. One longs for more meetings with the Diwan sahab.

On the fourth day, we proceeded from Bangalore to Pune. We are deeply indebted for the welcome extended to us by Srinivasraoji. He is a lean and thin man but lively to the core. He is a lawyer, a publisher, a writer, and the pillar of support for the campaign. He has recently launched a monthly series - *Book of Knowledge* in Kannada, of which perhaps the fourth issue has been brought out. The journal has a few blocks—

---

122. Pahalvan refers to someone who may be a body-builder, a weightlifter or a wrestler.
123. Mirza Ismail (1883-1959) served as the Diwan (equivalent to Prime Minister) of the states of Mysore, Jaipur, and Hyderabad.

including literature, science, history, geography, art, biology, botany—and contains essays useful for children. And it has been the writer's effort that the language used in the book is simple, animated, and interesting. There is no such series of books in the Hindi language. Srinivasrao is arranging for a similar publication in Hindi. He already has the sectional blocks; only the essays will have to be translated into readable Hindi. I hope that this series will find acceptance when published in Hindi. There are several books for children on fiction; there is however a considerable dearth of books to increase knowledge. This collection will remedy the lack.

[February-March 1935]

Translated by Trisha Lalchandani

30. An Important Proposal from the Sahitya Sammelan (*Sahitya Sammelan ka Ek Mahatvapoorna Prastava*)

The Sahitya Sammelan (Literary Convention), in accepting the proposal of planning the Akhil Bharatiya Sahityik Sabha or Mandal (All India Literary Council) has done an admirable job. There is urgent need for such a Council at the moment. When we have organisations for Science, Economics, History, and several others, the absence of a council of Indian literature was a significant lack. I hope that the proposal does not remain a mere ornament to the report but is made functional. Literary awakening is the prime marker of the life of a nation, and national language and literature can progress only when learned scholars from diverse regional languages come together to exchange ideas and instruct us in the progress of literature. The troubles in life, as in literature, are becoming more and more cumbersome, and to examine them from a national perspective has become difficult for the regions to do on their own. We get to know of literary developments in the world through English or other western languages; however, for making decisions regarding what portion of that is beneficial to the nation and what portion is best left out, it is necessary to have a responsible organisation.

It is ridiculous that we all stay like frogs in our wells in our provinces and every individual functions by themselves. The PEN-club, in creating a board of writers from the provinces, has tried to fill the lack to some degree, however, it is an international organisation, and it cannot fulfill our national needs. This body should also aim to conduct all its business in the national language. If learned men pen their thoughts in English and their thought also occurs in English, then the utility of the organisation will be nullified to a large extent. The wealth of the literature of our nation should come out to the world in the language of our nation, and it should get an appropriate place in world literature. Why is it necessary that when we have to face the world we should don the mantle of English? Initially, the practice of a national language will be difficult, however, one hopes that learned men in the provinces will adopt the national language keeping the good of the nation in view; a time will then come when they will be able to write in the national language and, it is only then, that the national language will become truly national.

[Editorial, *Hans*; May 1935]
Translated by Trisha Lalchandani

31. Hindi Sahitya-Sammelan in Indore (*Indore mein Hindi Sahitya-Sammelan*)

Shri Jainendra Kumar, discussing the Indore Sahitya Sammelan, has written the following in his letter:

> In my opinion, for the first time, this conference has been able to realise the essence of a national language conference. Hindi must now remain like the other regional languages; it will belong to the entire nation. The conference will also have to be similar to it.

If this work does not happen under the chairmanship of Gandhiji, then how else can it be completed? With relation to the style of joining words of Hindi with Hindustani, the conference explicitly put forth its views. A separate committee of learned men was set up for the script. The conference is yet to give a final word on the question of script. This is appropriate too. The committee of scholars will determine something after patiently studying all aspects of this issue. The conference has not deserted the question of the improvement and changes that need to be made in Hindi from the perspective of its proximity to and access by regional languages. Another important issue that has been discussed in the conference is the need for mutual introduction and exchange of ideas on those writers/ litterateurs who, through the medium of different languages, are producing literature which has the potential to be inter-provincial as well as Indian. Otherwise, how can there be unity in the life of the nation and its literature?

Why shouldn't the languages of the provinces and regions, while maintaining their heterogeneity and individuality, come together to assist in the development of a composite and a strong nation-state of India. This cannot be achieved through the medium of English. If it does happen, it will be incomplete. This conference has recognised the centrality of Hindi and has resolved to make it the medium through which all languages may come to be in touch and know each other.

A committee was formed under the coordinatorship of Bombay's Shri Munshi. I have had a long conversation with Shri Munshi about this. He is diligent as well as enterprising about it, and I believe, there will be some definitive result in the near future itself. Through the means of a proposal, it has been recommended that Hindi litterateurs be included in PEN, the international organisation for literature. All of this is the evidence of the expansion of views in favour of the conference and I welcome it.

The question that remains is whether contemporary literature in Hindi is worthy of being the national language or not, and in relation to this, I can say that the excellence of its contemporary literature is not the basis for Hindi to be the national language. Certainly, Rabindranath Tagore does not write in Hindi, however, Hindi should not feel ashamed of it. If Hindi has few competent people, there will be more, and if there are none, they will rise. Some may think of it as a misfortune on the part of Hindi, but I consider it fortunate, that Hindi belongs not to the wealthy, but to the peasants and workers. It is more the language of everyday life than the language of culture. If that is where the dignity of Hindi lies, it is also its strength. Today, the writer of Hindi cannot avoid noticing that the reader who reads and judges him is not only located in the vicinity but also in the far corners. Given this situation, it will not to be advantageous for writers of Hindi to remain extremely provincial, extremely communal, or parochial in their language or expression. Now, when the criterion for the national language becomes more and more distinct on an everyday basis, then the writers of Hindi will have to vigorously climb higher, else he will not be paid any attention. Hindi has effortlessly found the infallible means to give a progressive turn to literature and check its gathering lifelessness. I would request the awakened readers of other languages to not be completely dismissive of contemporary Hindi literature when they do not find satisfaction in it, but to have a little patience and if the number of such learned readers increase, then they will see that it will not take long for writers who can produce material akin to their taste. Today, I accept, there is little that is enduring in Hindi, but more of what has a short life. There is little in it that is superior, much of it is just ordinary; but will the speakers of other languages not give themselves a chance to acquire a flair in the language that sustains itself on the strength of peasants and workers?

That the Indore conference has made praiseworthy efforts in giving a national turn to script, language, and literature is undisputed. It has filled the deficit that had plagued people since long in organising an inter-provincial literary association, and if this attempt of ours is successful, our literature will truly become an asset for the nation. On behalf of this committee, Shri Kanhaiyalal Munshi has begun correspondence with the prominent literary figures of the provinces, and has recently sent a circular in which an effort to stabilise the style and structure of the association's programme has been made:

"Before the committee begins work on the election of the representatives of the various regional languages, it is essential that regional languages give sufficient thought to the central idea behind it. I, therefore, request you, to foster public opinion on it through a regional language newspaper which has sympathy for such an arrangement. I have full faith that following our regional languages, all nationalist newspapers will welcome this initiative. It is appropriate that for this purpose, one of the existing monthly journals be put to use, or a new journal be brought out, that has designated segments for each language, wherein, writers from regional languages write a piece for it every month, which gets published after being translated into Hindi. The writings should be brief but written by the best of scholars. Their topics could be:

1. A piece on any one constituent of the new literature in a particular regional language, such as, novel, drama, history, or an essay;

2. A piece on the monthly progress of the concerned regional language;

3. (a) Brief review of a novel or a play (b) a poem or two published in a newspaper or a journal of that month;

4. A critical piece on a literary composition of merit published in that month.

If you are unable to make arrangements for these pieces to be translated into Hindi, then some provision will be made for it in Bombay, as there we have the good fortune of having specialists of all languages. In this way we will have an inter-regional literary journal.

I will, therefore, request you to take the assistance of such litterateurs who wish to make this plan functional in your language and who will inform me that (1) you will ensure that this idea materialises and (2) you will send me some write-ups every month.

Please respond as promptly as possible so that I can give a report to Mahatmaji soon.

If the program put forth in this letter is brought into

practice, it will be of great service to the nation. A kind of cultural unity exists, in one way or the other, in the different regions of India from ancient times; however, it is surprising that when in today's age, multiple tools of unity are available, we are not even aware of one of the most important aspects of each other's culture. The literature of Russia and France, Sweden and Poland, Japan and Spain is made easily available to us through English. We read their writings, discuss them, and satisfy our literary appetite. Naturally, we desire to see the same excellence, the same vigour, the same talent in our literature too; and when on comparing, we find our literature from the provinces lacking, a sense of dismay and a feeling of inferiority strikes us; however, in reality, we are not even fully acquainted with the literature of our nation. The province is not the nation; the nation is the composite of all provinces. How can a national literature in its integrated form emerge until we are able to dismantle the biases that exist between different regional languages? The colours that we see at present, red, green, blue, yellow, it is only when they merge that they will acquire a vibrant glow. When a speaker sees a crowd of listeners swarming before him, it is almost as if Goddess Saraswati[124] has perched herself on his tongue; if the number of listeners dwindle, then the enthusiasm of the speaker diminishes in the same proportion. Similarly, when the genius of the writer writes with the sentiment of the entire nation, something extraordinary takes birth in it; ask the poet who might be writing a poem for the All-India Kavi Sammelan (All-India Poets' Convention)—his desire must be that he lavishes all the splendour of his soul on the poem. The vision of having expert poets sitting in front of him must be the whip that drives his talent. It is only in proportion to our responsibilities that the development of our strengths takes place. When, before the eyes of our litterateurs, not only their province but the entire nation is present, then, they will create literature with all their attention, preparedness, and ardent

124. Goddess of learning and the arts.

discipline. It isn't that he keeps something stowed away; rather the expansion of the field enlightens his intelligence in an imperceptible way. It is possible that even those learned men—who, on not having received much encouragement from the regional languages, do not make an effort to write, or write in English—may think of writing in the national language against their pride. I believe that the literary world of Hindi will salute this new progress and our respected editors will give life to this initiative through their criticism, advice, and good wishes.

[Editorial, *Hans*; June 1935]
Translated by Trisha Lalchandani

32. *Hans* in a New Form (*'Hans' Naye Roop Mein*)

If one had to write about the significance of a unified national literature after the current awakening with regard to national language, it would be a disgrace to the awakening. We all know how elevated the place of language and literature is among the constituents which make the nation. Thanks to the broad scope and the simplicity of Hindi, the nation has accepted it as its language and for eighteen years now a campaign for it has been running successfully in the entire country; now the time has come to take a step forward and reap the benefits to build a national literature on the ground prepared by the campaign for national language. This feeling had risen in the hearts of quite a few gentlemen over these years, however the guiding forces required to make it practical were not found. This year, the proposal of this intent was finalised at the Indore Sahitya Sammelan, whose chairperson was Mahatma Gandhi; it is he who had initiated the campaign for national language eighteen years ago, and made the effort to integrate India's literature from the provinces. In all different aspects of life and culture, All-India institutions are present, however owing to the diversity of languages, there is still no such literary institution. After crossing the deep divide that exists between languages, the right time to work for literary coordination has arrived.

The completion of this goal requires such a monthly newspaper which would publish writings from the established writers of all the provinces, such that there is exchange between the languages to bring about promotion and progression of national literature. It is in this manner that literature will beget such a temperament which will eventually bring about development of the Rashtriya Sahitya Parishad (National Literary Council).

Hence, I have decided that from the following October, the well-known magazine *Hans* shall be published in a new format. *Hans*, now, will now be managed and published by a private limited company, which has been set up precisely for this purpose. Every month, it will have a hundred pages and its annual subscription will be Rs. 5. Obtaining writings from the scholars and established writers, getting them translated into Hindi, striving to render every aspect of its literary style is painstaking as well as expensive. We have had to arrange for able translators to translate ten or twelve regional literary writings and quite a few supporters, with the sentiment of sacrifice, have promised to help us. The enthusiasm with which the lovers of national literature in each of the provinces have welcomed this initiative, has made us hopeful. We believe that the talented writers of the nation as well as readers will encourage us with their support. It is only then that the indifference and disinterest that one province has with the literature of another province will be banished. We are glad that we received the support of Gujarat's foremost litterateur, Shriyut Kanhaiyalal Munshi, in editorial work—considered to be the initiator of such a discourse.

There is no need to write just how important the work is. We dream of a future where the when the writings of renowned writers of India will be relished between one end of the country to the other and the entire nation will be proud of them. It is only then that our literature will gain even more respect in the literary world across the globe, and it will also play a role in the cultural development of the world. It is possible to surmise the quality of the magazine for which the literary genius of the entire nation will provide assistance.

We consider it appropriate to settle all doubts, which, have unfortunately assailed the minds of some gentlemen. Though our efforts have been welcomed all over, there are still a few great intellectuals who keep reiterating that when we can function through the means of English language, what is the need for acquainting ourselves with the national language. They are of the opinion that the farce of national literature has been erected only as a means to establish the rule of Hindi over other regional languages. We would like to humbly declare that our intention is not to cause impairment to regional languages, but to build national literature with its support. To chop off the branch on which we are perched will be giving an example of our own foolishness. Of course, we accept that we take the knowledge of the national language by each and every person in the nation as mandatory, otherwise, how would it be a national language; however, there is no possibility of it causing any harm to other languages. Whatever is their field of operation, will remain the same; but, yes, the scope for attaining fame will widen for talented writers. If this causes damage to the language, then we cannot ascertain what will profit it. To the supporters of English, what else can I say but that after spending billions of rupees we have not been able to make even a single person out of a hundred capable of reading and understanding English, and the wealth required to teach English to the entire country is beyond the capacity of this poor nation.

[Editorial, *Hans*; July 1935]
Translated by Trisha Lalchandani

33. Association for Indian Literature (*Bhartiya Sahitya ka Sangathan*)

Recently, Shri Kanhaiyalal Ji Munshi[125] wrote a thought-provoking piece on this question for the English papers, in which he has endeavoured to show how and in what form a national association for inter-state literatures should be made. I will provide an independent translation of the piece:

'For some time now, literary awareness is being generated in all those provinces that possess a language of their own. The outcome of this has been that small literary societies have come up in every region, and they have become part of regional literary councils. However, in most cases, these societies are working in their own different directions. No mutual exchange happens among them. To the extent that the amount of knowledge we have of the literary and cultural works of England, we do not possess of the literature of our neighbouring regions. Outside each region are very few people who have any awareness of the genres and style, or the literary trends of budding writers. In places where Hindi is not spoken, people might be acquainted with the names of Tulsi or Surdas, but they are oblivious to the literary production that is being done in Hindi. Whatever familiarity we have with Bangla literature is only with the compositions of Rabindranath Tagore. Whatever we know about Gujarati literature is through the English translation of Mahatmaji's autobiography. The Romantic literature (Anand Lakshmi) that new Gujarat has developed is inaccessible to people of other regions. The new literature that is being created in the regions of Karnataka, Tamil Nadu, Andhra, Kerala, is unknown to the inhabitants who live to the north of the river Godavari.

'But the predominance of the national-sentiment/patriotism on contemporary literature exists, and will continue to do so. All regional literary works are gradually progressing towards a larger national unity, and if India wishes to achieve its nationality in a holistic manner, then a national literary association is absolutely necessary, in which each province provides its contribution. However, such an association is possible only

125. Shri Kanhaiyalal Munshi (1887-1971) was a writer and an independence movement activist.

through the medium of Hindi, in which the writers from all provinces sincerely provide their contributions in a united manner. Only then will we be successful in establishing an association of regional literary councils, which will be an All-India Literary Association. This thought has been taking shape in my mind from 1935, when I had gone to take active part in the Gujarati literary council.

'In the Hindi Sahitya Sammelan that was presided over by Mahatma Gandhi last April, this plan was accepted. From the conversations I had with other literary figures, I came to know that similar thoughts have been there in the minds of many others, and the time is now ripe to make efforts in this direction. Mahatmaji himself agreed to guide the programme to bring together different regional representatives through the medium of Hindi. Generally it is understood that if such a programme becomes successful, then in one form or the other, an inter-regional literary society will come into being. The following resolutions were taken in this conference:

'With the intention of establishing mutual relations among the literary contributors from various regions of the country, and garnering their contributions for the task of evolving the Hindi language, this conference has formed a committee of the following gentlemen, and extends to them the right to add new members if required:

Shriyut Kanhaiyalal Maniklal Munshi
Shri Harihar Sharma
Pandit Girdhar Sharma

'The aforementioned committee shall elect new members, and after the initial proceedings, shall begin their work.

'Firstly, to bring regional literatures together, it was thought that either a contemporary monthly journal in Hindi be used as a platform, or a new journal be taken out in which space is reserved for literature from each region. Regional scholars should write for the journal, which would be published after getting translated into Hindi. In this way, the following topics will be covered on a monthly basis:

Succinct commentaries on the literary and cultural events in each region;

A brief history of the development of regional literatures, with special focus on the progress of modern literatures, and the feeling of nationalism they generate;

Bhaav-geet or lyric poetry composed in various regional languages;

Short stories of high literary merit that are part of regional literatures;

(Gradually) novels;

Familiarising regional folk-literatures;

One-act plays;

Detailed vignettes of major poets and established writers of every regional folk-literature, along with a literary appreciation of their art;

Overviews of different established regional literary writers in all languages;

A comparative understanding of different literary and cultural trends in the regions;

Literary reviews of books to be published in different regional languages;

Hindi translations of extracts from contemporary literatures to be published in various regional journals;

Brief commentaries related to literatures in foreign languages;

Abridged translations of classic novels published in regional languages;

Debates related to the national script.

In short, this monthly journal will bridge the gap that is being felt these days for an All-India Literary journal which can become the central organ. To successfully carry out this task, there is a need for cooperation between all major literary writers of the various regions, literary councils, and other literary bodies, especially nationalist newspapers is absolutely crucial. To ensure the success of this endeavour, firstly it is required to prepare a favourable ground, and a few literary contributors in each region are required who are passionate for this cause. Therefore, through this letter, I urge and plead for the cooperation of those literary councils, literary organisations and contributors of people's literature, who are committed to this cause.

'In the past, the Aryan culture diligently erased regional

boundaries and, despite the differences in language and script, had made full efforts to establish literary and cultural unity. In contemporary culture, the easy availability of amenities and conveniences, and the kiss of life that the nationalist sentiment gives to political life, will very soon result in propagating cultural unity, and in a short time span of 10-20 years only, we will witness the dawn of an ever-expanding national language and the establishment of a mutual association between regional literatures, in which each province will offer one of their unparalleled literary creations as a gift.'

[Editorial, *Hans*; July 1935]
Translated by Sarah Mariam

34. A Critique of the Indian Literary Association (*Bhartiya Sahitya ke Sangathan ki Ek Aalochana*)

It must be known to the readers of *Hans* that in the previous month, Shriyukt Kanhaiyalal Munshi published a pamphlet titled 'Bharatiya Sahitya ka Sangathan' (Indian Literary Association), in which he expressed the need for such a magazine in Hindi and also proposed a scheme for the same wherein on the issue of regional literature, the writings by the regional scholars of Hindi are published, and through the medium of Hindi, a space is created, which would facilitate the readers of different provinces, as well as acquaint the readers of Hindi with them, and the best that emerge from various literatures of the nation, are not limited to staying within the province, but can reach the entire country. Our friend Shriyukt Chandraguptji Vidyalankar[126] has expressed the following doubts in a thoughtful piece in the August issue of *Vishal Bharat*:

1) As litterateurs whose writings will be published in the magazine will not fully know what shape their creation will take after their translation in Hindi, though an author might send some write-up for such a magazine as an act of charity, or feeling bound on request or owing to some kind of inspiration,

126. Shriyukt Chandraguptji Vidyalankar (1906-1982) was a Hindi short-story writer and playwright.

they cannot have any vital interest in the magazine. The consequence will be that such a magazine, very soon, will become second grade and after some time, third grade.

2) Through the magazine, the Hindi world will get a second-hand flavour of the writings in other regional languages, but how will the people of other provinces get acquainted with the litterateurs of the entire nation?
3) What will a lone magazine do in this regard; it is similar to the work of a campaign, and from this perspective, it will be good if an endeavour is made by all the Hindi magazines and newspapers, and why only Hindi, but all the magazines and newspapers of entire Bharatvarsha (India) be filled with this idea that they must make the maximum effort to acquaint their readers with the writings from other regions and provinces.
4) In the end, he has expressed the need for a Rashtriya Sahitya Parishad (National Literary Council) and has emphasised that first such a Parishad be created, and a full-fledged literary magazine be published by it.

I felt glad on reading this observation of Chandraguptji's. This tells us that intellectuals are giving this issue a thought, which is far better than accepting things blindly or becoming indifferent straightaway. Even while comprehending the significance of Bhai Chandraguptji's doubts, I propose:

The writings of litterateurs that we intend to publish, will be acquired from them directly for *Hans* and we will try to make them send their writings after having them translated into Hindi or write in Hindi directly (if they have acquired the knowledge of it). If neither of the two is possible, then we will get their writings translated. We will try to get fresh write-ups from them and the ones, which have specifically been written for us. There is no reason why when they give their writings to magazines in their own languages, they should not give them to *Hans*, which aims to have their writings reach the entire nation. I am of the opinion that established writers of Bangla, Marathi, and other languages will also not dislike it if their writings are published in a magazine that aims to reach people of all accomplished languages and is assiduous in wanting to achieve it. For example, consider the writers in Hindi. If Bhai Chandraguptji believes that

> if sending his piece to such and such magazine will land him in the hands of the lovers of national language all over Bharat (India), then, I believe, he will write for such a magazine. In such a situation, I do not see any reason as to why *Hans* should not receive excellent contributions and, as a consequence, turn out to be a substandard journal.

The Hindi world can now not only have access to second hand, but even third, fourth and fifth hand content of English, French or any other languages of Europe; however when we shall take that content directly from the writer and will try that it should have been written solely for *Hans*, then the content will be first hand instead of second. *Hans* will be in service of those residents of one province who might have the desire to be acquainted with the literature of another province. If a Gujarati reader wanted to know something in relation to literature in Telugu now, he would not have any means for it. Once *Hans* is published, this desire of his will be easily fulfilled. Similarly, it will become extremely easy for literature lovers from all provinces to gain acquaintance with literatures from other provinces through *Hans*.

Hans is precisely that endeavour which our brother wished to make, to suffuse a certain kind of sentiment in the magazines and newspapers all over Bharat (India). All magazines publish fiction, therefore, no magazine should be devoted purely to fiction—that cannot be its design. Political write-ups are given alongside others in all magazines however there are also some magazines which publish only political pieces. By issuing a magazine with this aim, we wish to bring literatures of all regions close to one another, and in our limited perspective, this could be the foundation of national literature.

Towards the end, I only want to propose that establishing the Rashtriya Sahitya Parishad (National Literary Council) is on my mind, and this magazine is preparing the ground for the same. First let the feeling of nationalism colour our literary sensibilities; how would it then take to establish such a Council? Representatives of all regional languages have been put forth in the advisory committee of *Hans*, and I hope that it will become a board soon. I assure Chandraguptji and all lovers of literature that *Hans* will be a pure literary magazine, as is clearly evident from the list of esteemed personalities who are its founding pillars. Its chief function is service of literature. Who will deny that campaigning is also a part of one's service to literature? I request Bhai Chandragupt for his support in this good work. Goals, his and mine are the same, only the means differ; however all good works commence with a dream. If there were no dreamers, the world would be barren then.

[Editorial, *Hans*; August-September 1935]
Translated by Trisha Lalchandani

35. The New Form of *Hans* (*Hans* ka Naya Roop)

Six years from this day, from the first date of its inception, *Hans* has endeavored to give a monthly update to its readers on the progress of developments in other Indian languages. However, due to lack of resources, it has not been able to achieve the success it desired, though this objective has always been foremost on its agenda. One does not become a nation by virtue of being part of the same country; rather, one becomes a nation through an insuppressible steadfast, cultural unity. Script, language and literature are integral aspects of culture. The nation has decided the question of the script and it has been resolved that the Nagari script would be adopted for the national language. Now there is no difference of opinion pertaining to the issue of language as well. It has been decided that Hindustani will be our national language. We would now like to complete the process by bridging the lacunae in our attempt at cultural unification by transforming the narrow, regional or provincial character of our literature to the broad domain of the national. The entire nation is unable to benefit from the font of that elixir of the numinous intellectual spirit which seems to be encompassing the entire nation uniformly at this moment as its flow gets impeded owing to linguistic differences. If Bharat (India) has to attain a full-fledged spirit of nationalism then she has to build literary associations to propagate Indian literature. *Hans* has undertaken on itself this significant task. From the 1st of October, *Hans* would be published in the form of a national organ of Indian literatures. There would be 112 pages in it; its annual subscription charge would be six rupees and six-monthly subscription would be three rupees fifty paisa. It would be edited by Shriyukt Kanhaialal Munshi and me. We are trying to get the support of all famous literary personalities of India for it. Mahatma Gandhi has blessed us. It is but true that owing to his inspiration that this task was undertaken. For the publication of *Hans*, a public limited company was created in Bombay (Mumbai) and from now on, it will look after its publication.

Hans would be published like before, from the *Hans* office in Benaras. One of its offices is also there at 111, Esplanade Road, Bombay (Mumbai). We have made this arrangement only with the objective of serving the cause of national language and national literature. We do not have any vested business interest in it and so we hope that our beloved readers would continue to be committed to *Hans* like before and not let its price hike of two and a half rupees alienate them from it. Considering the magnitude of the great task before us, this rise in its price is not much really. Just imagine how much effort and investment needs to be made now as well as in future, in order to present in Hindi different pieces from languages like Kannada, Tamil, Telugu, Bangla, Marathi, Gujarati, Urdu and others. You would be acquainted with literatures from all over India through *Hans*. Whatever is powerful and pleasing in different regional literatures would be made available to you by *Hans*. Like in the past, rare and remarkable Hindi literary compositions would be presented in it along with it all. Is it not a matter of regret that we are till date not apprised of the diverse streams and their developments in our literatures from the regions? We are quite familiar with ancient Bangla literature. But we are quite unaware of its progress in contemporary times. We are totally ignorant of the literatures of southern India. When India is one nation, Hindi is the national-script, then whatever is forthcoming in the literatures of India, becomes national literature. Then only shall we develop a literary perspective and we can measure literature using the national yardstick, and our literary goals and ideals will be enhanced. By continuing to be a subscriber of *Hans,* do not think that your responsibilities for building a national literature is over. Try to make efforts for publicising *Hans* and through it, be committed as a proud participant in this cultural *yagya*[127]. When the gentlefolk from other linguistic communities are showing such enthusiasm for the cause of national language and making arrangements for funds for the publication of *Hans* and well-known writers and authors in other languages are giving such liberal inputs, then will our readers, who have shown their passion for literature by continuing to subscribe to *Hans* for so many years, will not motivate us with their love for national literature? We sincerely thank all our esteemed benefactors, who have helped us to propagate this idea.

[Editorial, *Hans;* August-September 1935]
Translated by Anuradha Ghosh

36. Why should one remove the "shirorekha"[128] in the script? (*Shirorekha Kyon Hatni Chahiye?*)

One becomes hopeful that perhaps in the near future, we would be able to attain our goal considering the enthusiasm and competence with which the Nagari Lipi Samiti (Nagari Script Council) has begun to complete its difficult responsibilities. And it is indeed delightful that there was not much opposition to the proposals and orders of the Samiti, though there was a lot of apprehension regarding it. National integration is so dear to us that we are prepared to accept whatever suggestions

127. Fire sacrifice.
128. 'shirorekha' – upstroke, or the line used on top of an alphabet in Hindi Devanagari script.

are relevant to it. The proposal pertaining to the question of 'shirorekha' or upstrokes on the letters of the written script has been almost accepted by all owing to the beautiful manner in which the Samiti has dealt with it. Upstrokes are not an important part of Nagari alphabets. The Brahmi alphabets from which Nagari letters have evolved has led to the development of Bangla, Tamil, Gujarati and others; but 'shirorekha' or upstrokes are not there in any script except in Nagari. We have become habituated into marking of 'shirorekhas' since childhood and our pens involuntarily, almost by force, inevitably traces the upper line on the head of the alphabet, but through practice one can control the movement of the pen. There is no doubt in this that by giving up the 'shirorekha' we can increase the speed of our writing and our complaint of it being slow too would then be resolved, and printing it would become easier. It is beside the point that now the issue of letters without their 'shirorekhas' would appear somewhat bald and headless, is largely an emotional one. When our eyes become used to upstroke-less alphabets, then those very same letters would appear beautiful and we would be surprised that why for several millennia we had been carrying such an utterly useless burden.

[Editorial, *Hans*; October 1935]
Translated by Anuradha Ghosh

37. Unity of Regional Literatures (*Prantiya Sahitya ki Ekta*)

Hans, infused as it is with such a grand and lofty ideal, harbouring the desire of being the central literary organ of the nation, is being brought out today. Its main goal is to present before Bharat (India) national integration of diverse provinces through the national language Hindi.

The nation is not an object, it is an idea. Several crores of men and women have endeavoured resolutely to realise this idea. Today, innumerable Indians have articulated it in their thought and practice. The entire 'Hind' is one and indivisible.

This feeling manifests itself in various shapes and forms.

People literate in English express these feelings in English, and many others in their mother tongue. Many efforts are being made in the same direction. They cannot take one form in the absence of a national language and literature.

Now we have sworn to establish Hindi as the national language. However this language cannot be the language of everyday transaction and oral use only; it should also be a language for literature. This language should be used for cultural exchange and aesthetic philosophy as well. If India is one and undivided, then its cultural exchange and aesthetic philosophy should be expressed in the same language, through an inter-dependent flow of literary practices.

No matter what India's national language is, we need to draw in elements from all country languages to strengthen it. Let Indian literature be such that it is aesthetically embellished by all the essential universal elements of literatures of the provinces and regions. Literature should be such that everyone gets a glimpse of the soul of the nation through it. It is this thought which is the inspiration behind our efforts.

There is an inner unity among the literatures of all the provinces of the country. Irrespective of which language the literary compositions have been written in, they have all been woven with the same thread. This thread is not a new one, it has continued through tradition. All literature is inspired by Bhagwan Vyasa Krishna Dwaipayan.[129] Flashes of the unparalleled beauty of the *Ramayana* are reflected in them. The resonance of the *Puranas* echoes through the literature of all ages. The light shown by the creators of Sanskrit literature has encouraged litterateurs from each region. Our fiction too, taking on the shape of a coordinated whole, has linked together literature from each region. *The Jataka Tales*[130] are found in one form or the other in all regional literatures. Gunadhya's

129. Vyasa, sometimes called Krishna Dwaipayan, is considered to be the compiler of the Mahabharata.

130. The Jataka Tales are a compilation of stories surrounding the birth and life of Gautama Buddha.

Brihatkatha[131] and translations of *The Panchatantra*[132] have been lovingly adopted by all regions. Our folktales are self-generated and eternal in nature and their essential elements are present in the collective cultural imagination of the land and the people.

In the previous era, *bhagwat-dharma* (relation between God and execution of our duties) and *bhagwat-bhakti* (relation between God and our devotion for Him) gave a new lease of life to literature from each and every province. The powerful doctrines of Vidyapati[133] and Chandidas,[134] Soor[135] and Tulsi,[136] Narsi,[137] Meera[138] and Kabir,[139] Gyandev[140] and Sadhu Tukaram,[141] Ramanuja,[142] Madhva Vallabh[143] and Chaitanya,[144] on the one hand, call attention to the cultural unity of India, and, on the other, unifies the practice of rites and rituals all across the country.

And, which region was not affected by the Hindu-Muslim

---

131. Brihatkatha, attributed to Gunadhya, is an ancient Indian epic in the Paiśācī language.
132. The *Panchatantra* is a collection of fables originally composed in Sanskrit.
133. Vidyapati (1352-1448) was a Maithili poet.
134. Chandidas (b. 1408 CE) was a poet from Bengal.
135. Soor (1478-1573) was a devotional poet known for his lyrics written in praise of Lord Krishna.
136. Tulsidas (1511-1623), a saint and a poet, is best known as the author of *Ramcharitmanas,* a retelling of the Ramayana (in Sanskrit) in Awadhi.
137. Narsi was a fifteenth century Vaishnava poet from Gujarat.
138. Meera (1498-1546) was a poet belonging to the Bhakti tradition.
139. Kabir was a fifteenth century mystic poet and saint.
140. Gyandev (1275-1296), or Dnyaneshwar, was a thirteenth century Marathi poet and saint.
141. Sadhu Tukaram was a seventeenth century Hindu poet and saint.
142. Ramanuja (1017-1137) was a Vaishnavite Hindu philosopher.
143. Madhva Vallabha (1238-1317), or Madhvacharya, was a Hindu philosopher and a proponent of the Dvait Vedanta.
144. Chaitanya (1486-1534) was a Hindu mystic and saint.

exchange of rites and ritual practices during the time of Muslim rule? If Muslims adopted the vocabulary and *rasa* (emotion) of the Hindus in matters of music, then there was a propagation of their vocabulary in matters related to the state and its policies. Both of them together created the Hindustani language, which is our national language today; and the first Hindustani poet is Khusro, who was the contemporary of Balban.[145] His riddles, verse, and *mukrian* are the wealth of the Hindi language even today, and none equal to him has yet been born. For centuries, cultural exchanges have taken place. The Hindu poets would write poetry in Persian and then in Urdu, and the Muslim poets would write in Hindi. Hindi still feels proud of those Muslim poets who composed verses in Hindi, and wrote commentaries on the verse epics. Jayasi's *Padmavat* is still a matter of pride for the Hindi language, and which language was not influenced by the stream of love and unity which the Sufi poets initiated by severing the deadlock between sects and faith? It will be impossible to assess the contribution made by the various groups of people today in constructing the form that our culture and tradition has assumed in association with the centuries of the past.

After the arrival of the British, the ideals of literature have been moulded according to literatures in English. Essays, novels, stories, plays and poetry, has been enriched by the Sanskrit literature of Bana,[146] Magha,[147] and Kalidas,[148] however their form, finesse, and humour, has evolved from the hearts of the poets fashioned out of the Romantic movement, popular in England. They have found their inspiration in Shelley, Wordsworth, Scott, and Lytton.

A reflection of the trail of blazing nationalism pervades all

---

145. Ghiyas ud din Balban who reigned from 1266 to 1287 was the ruler of the Mamluk dynasty of Delhi.
146. Banabhatta was a seventh century Sanskrit poet.
147. Magha was an eighth century Sanskrit poet.
148. Kalidas was a classical Sanskrit writer from the fourth-fifth century.

literatures as it was transmitted into our lives after the division of Bengal in 1904. Today, literary development is led by the inspirational force of the writings and speeches of Mahatma Gandhi and also the creations of the poet Rabindranath Tagore.

There was and still is fundamental unity within Indian literature, only the garb of language has remained distinct. If all of literature could be accessed by all Indians in one place in one language, then, surely, this unity will fortify and attain form. The gathering of literature of all regions in one place and in one language will lend each literature vigour and momentum. Some people harbour the fear that this reveals the symptoms of the destruction of regional pride, but if given a careful thought, this fear seems unfounded. If, regional literatures, standing at par with each other, measure and assess each other, and in correspondence with each other find new directives, inspiration, and vitality, how will this harm any literature? Today, if our literature seems to be shrinking, it will move upstream. Kalidas, Homer, Goethe, or Shelley merely imparts lessons in humour. Till the peripheries of our regional literature broaden, it will not be able to find its due place in world literature. Therefore, there is no doubt that as a consequence of these efforts, instead of shrinking, literature will attain wholesomeness and character.

Some litterateurs ask, why such efforts in Hindi? Why not in English?

I am confounded and saddened that the afore-mentioned awkward question could be still asked in 1935. Does this country no longer have the strength and has love for the nation become so weak that India should feel compelled to find expression through a foreign language? And, if this is correct, then we should feel deeply ashamed. English is a beautiful language; its literature has an immortal sweetness; a lot of our modern literature has been created, because of being inspired by it; but how many understand this language? How can this language portray our customs and traditions? How can we present our traditions that are deeply tied to our country language through an ill-fitting structure of a foreign tongue?

Hindi is the older sibling of many regional languages. It shares a close relationship with Urdu. Many crores of our people speak Hindi, and a larger number can understand it. Today, it has been seated on the nation's throne by the makers of the nation. Should we abandon this and allow literary exchange in a foreign tongue?

No other language but Hindi, can belong to this nation. The sooner we accept this material reality and believe in this fact, the sooner shall good fortune dwell over our nation.

If the literature of all regions is embodied in Hindi, then it will not be the Hindi of Prayag or Kashi; it will surely embody the attributes of all regions. There will be variety in its sentence construction. New words from unfamiliar languages will be added to its lexicon. All such elements will together make the national language.

For a language as catholic as this, it is important that only elementary Hindi be used. That simple words should comprise the language is desirable, but I do understand that from a literary perspective, this will not be an easy task. Today, elements from Sanskrit are rapidly increasing in Hindi, Bangla, Marathi, Gujarati, Telugu and Malayalam. If it were not for the wealth and beauty of Sanskrit, the progress of these languages would not have been possible, which implies that this issue presents itself to several litterateurs as they try to preserve its wealth, sweetness and simplicity. They know these difficulties well; they will not get resolved so easily. There is a question greater and more significant than this? In which language should literature be composed that it is understood both by Hindus and Muslims? In the market, during festivities, in daily usage, simple Hindi can come close to simple Urdu, however, when we talk about literary eloquence, poetry, intense and meaningful renderings, this language falls short gravely. Every writer will take necessary and anticipated nourishment from their most loved contributions. There is no scope for dejection here. We can be liberated only after the generation of one literary language for Hindus and Muslims. Neither of the two should omit nor lose their personality; instead they must embrace the other's characteristics to create a new language.

It needs as much magnanimity as it does patience. All the objects of worth in the world are generated only after a long investment of time and herculean efforts.

[Editorial, *Hans*; October 1935]
Translated by Trisha Lalchandani

38. Our Humble Appeal to *Triveni* (*'Triveni' se Hamara Namra Nivedan*)

Our companion, the English journal *Triveni* published from Madras, welcoming our organisation of Indian literary association and *Hans* wrote a brief note, which is being presented below[149]. Our companion has from the very

149. "A COMMONWEALTH OF LITERATURES

We welcome the efforts that are being made by Mr. K.M. Munshi to give an all-India status to our provincial literatures. *Hans*, the Hindi magazine till now conducted by Shri Premchandji, will hereafter be edited conjointly by Sjts, Munshi and Premchandji. It will publish articles about the different literatures, with personal sketches of writers and poets, and translations into Hindi of the more valuable literary pieces. *Triveni* has similar aims, and since 1928, it has bestowed a great deal of attention on the literary and cultural movements in Andhra, Maharashtra, Karnataka, and other linguistic units of India. In fact, this has been a prominent feature of *Triveni*, and its not quite accurate today to say that 'we know the latest literary and cultural activity in England, but not that of our neighbouring province'.

While we readily recognise that it is useful to conduct a magazine in Hindi for the benefit of all Indian province (sic.). We believe that it is not less important that Indian literature should keep in touch with the literature of the world by the publication of articles on the Indian literatures and translations of poems, plays and stories in an international language like English. There are many ways in which Treveni (sic.) and *Hans* can cooperate with advantage. There is however, a wide spread feeling in

beginning upheld the ideal of cultural unity of India and has quite efficiently observed the same. *Hans* too has this very objective. The difference is only this that while *Triveni* adopts the medium of English as it desires to portray Indian culture and literature in the international arena, *Hans* supports the notion of national culture and literature and thereby strives to create an affinity between the different literatures of India and by erasing cultural differences it aims to delineate the form that this might assume. Our opinion is that till we do not have one literature and till we have some kind of uniformity and similitude in our culture, in our present state with all our differences, we will not attain any recognition or respect in the international sphere. Till we decide the national goal for our literature and culture, we cannot aspire to be accepted at the international level.

Nationalism alone paves the way to internationalism. We can reach our desired destination by using this intermediate step like a ladder. Till Indian literatures become aware of each other, the proposition that it will be internationally recognised, is almost like saying that even before India gains her independence, she will demand to be a member,

---

South India that, in their zeal for the propagation of Hindi, the pracharaks are making exaggerated claims on its behalf, and referring to the literatures in Kannada, Tamil or Telugu with condescension. It is one thing to say that, as Hindi is spoken by the largest number of Indians, it might eventually serve as a medium of communication between province and province. It is altogether different to exalt it to the position of a national language and impose it on all provinces, to the deteriment (sic.) of the local language. We draw a distinction between a common language and a national language. There are several subnationalities in India, and to them their mother-tongue is the national language and also the prime vehicle of creative self-expression. Hindi is not inherently superior to Telugu or Bengali; nor is its literature as rich and varied as theirs. We respectfully warn Mr. Munshi against the subtle danger that lurks behind the Hindi movement. The *Hans* must steer clear of it." (p. 205)

in the comity of nations. Nationhood is impossible to attain without fulfilling all the criterion that defines a nation and a state, and in a country, where thoughts on nationalism is so chaotic, disparate and disorganised, it would not be much of a surprise to see, that the effort to scale international heights, come crashing down, head over heels, in utter futility. If different sub-nations continue to exist in India, and each one continues to preserve the differences of one's literature and culture with reference to others, and not make any effort to interact mutually, then there would be no development of the sense of nationhood till doomsday. We need to somewhat abandon our ties to our regions and provinces.

If by chance political unity is attained without cultural unity, such a unity can never be a permanent one. If the Hindi *pracharaks* (campaigners) are making the mistake of trying to prove the supremacy of Hindi over Tamil or other languages, then one has to condone it. Till they have faith in the supremacy of their objective, why should they sacrifice their time and wits for it? After subscribing to a new perspective, we do get slightly arrogant in our attitude. This is but natural. The learned should consider this to be juvenile enthusiasm.

Hindi is not impatient to become the national language. In order to mentally reconcile, if one imagines that there is a difference between 'Common language' and 'National language', then I have no objection. We desire to make Hindustani a 'Common language' and our objective is simply this that 'It might eventually serve as a Medium of Communication between province and province.' It is due to this, that Hindi cannot be considered as just another language, whose literature, is superior to Telugu or Bangla, or a dozen other literatures, but because it is understood and spoken by most people. We therefore need the medium of Hindi to create some kind of literary unity. What one fails to understand till now is how can this arrangement then harm provincial languages and literatures? Does this in any way offend any literature if its circle of readership widens and it gets an opportunity to acquaint itself with other literatures?

Does this hurt the good poets and writers of Telugu or Tamil if the entire nation rather than a region benefits from their compositions and does it bode evil to the readership in these languages if they get an opportunity to enjoy the pleasures of reading other great literatures? We get acquainted with world literatures through English and English literature--does this impair us in any way? If this does not harm us, then how can it be detrimental if one is introduced to other Indian literatures? Or is the cause of privation due to the use of Hindi, considered to be a poor language as a medium rather than English? If this enterprise was in English then would it have been more satisfactory to our companion? Is it possible to attain a literary integration through any other language? If not, then what great crime has Hindi committed in making this effort? For an international demeanour we surely need to study English; for provincial usage, the mother tongue is always there; but for a national deportment it has become important for us to learn Hindi. Perhaps we can still sneer at Hindi now, but there will come a time when we can no longer hold it in contempt.

[Editorial, *Hans*; November 1935]
Translated by Anuradha Ghosh

39. Indian Literature and Pt. Jawaharlal Nehru (*Bhartiye Sahitya Aur Pt. Jawaharlal Nehru*)

It was on those very days when the necessity of organising an Indian literary association with some satisfactory objectives was being discussed on the pages of *Hans*, sitting in the Almora jail, Pandit Jawaharlalji too was contemplating, quite independently, in the very same direction on this issue. Though he had no clue about our preparations for it, his views on the issue published as a write-up quite recently in the fraternal journal *Pratap* shows a surprising similarity. What is evident from this is the gathering momentum of the rhythm in which national consciousness and opinions on cultural unity is making a head way. Nehruji is the life of the nation and his heart is the heart of the nation, and in it is reflected the complete sentiments and aspirations of the people. Literary and cultural unity of a nation is an integral aspect of its progress and development; strengthening of such thought is a propitious sign as it augurs well for the future of the country.

Nehruji has rightly pointed out at the very beginning of the piece that owing to historical and geographical factors, new literature in Hindi seems to be impoverished, as it was first Bengal, and then Maharashtra and Gujarat that developed as they were influenced by Western thought. Owing to delayed political consciousness in Hindi-speaking provinces and the diversity of languages in the country, no immediate advantage could be gained from the awakening in other regions; and if we are not making a mistake, then those Indian languages that are considered well developed, when compared with the developed languages of the world, appear trivial and insignificant. One of the principal causes for this is that even today our fascination for English has not reduced one bit and the entire genius of the country is spent on the mastering of it; the shoulders that bear the burden of developing this nation, neglect their own languages, considering them inferior. The second reason is that the exchanges between regional languages have almost come to a halt and one can say that the nation's literature is progressively becoming weak and lifeless, locked as they are, in different ware-houses and chambers, owing to the lack of free play of wind and light. Hence,

> We need to benefit from this experience and try to build some kind of a relation between the different languages of the country. An association of regional language litterateurs must be made and they should have occasional meetings. This would help our literatures to develop and in place of rivalry and bitterness, it would foster friendly cooperation. Opinions and perspectives would rapidly spread all across the country and this would strengthen our unity. Though I have heard that efforts are underway to begin this process, but I do not know much about it. I hope that such an Indian Literary Association will invite all

> languages across India. Hindi and Urdu are not sisters; they are two faces on one body. We have to build a close and intimate bond between the two. Bangla, Marathi and Gujarati are the younger sisters of Hindi; the languages of the south are the oldest in our country. Apart from this, one should be taking all minor and major languages into this association. I would like to recommend that English too is included in this. Though English is not our language, it still has a great role in shaping the life of this nation. It is almost like a language that has a step-sisterly relation.

In my opinion, the role of English has become so crucial that it needs no help from any association or institution. It is not a linguistic co-wife, but it is the queen of all languages; all other Indian languages are dependent on her kind benevolence. The condition of our educated segment is such that they cannot write a line correctly in their mother tongue. It is sad that most of them who are acknowledged as our leaders are inexperienced in their mother tongue; one can see with one's own eyes the fate of such a society in which leaders are so far removed from their people that they have no link with their language. And to add to it, we are not even ashamed of our incapabilities and inexperiences, which might indicate some hope for the future. We bluntly declare with pride and boldness that we are more comfortable speaking and writing in English.

Going ahead with it Nehruji has affirmed that Hindi must become the national language and Marathi, Bangla, Gujarati, Gurmukhi, etcetera should be written in the Hindi script and it is on this premise that the campaign for propagating Hindi is based. After all this you say:

> The other question is that our litterateurs must establish relationships with litterateurs of the world and be members of international literary associations. Without this we cannot be considered as members of leading nations. We must acknowledge that in this new age[150], fresh ideas and perspectives are coming

150. 'Navayug', literally, new age, indicates renaissance.

> from Europe and America. Without engaging with them, we cannot confront the world in our times. The first thing that this new age teaches us is that we cannot make different fragments of this world as it is one whole and those who want to disassociate from it will lag behind.

These words are literally true; but to participate in international associations we have to take recourse to one national language. We cannot enter the international arena on the strength of our regional languages. To dream that all regional languages of India can acquire the status of the developed languages of the world is a fallacy. One nation can take only one language to represent themselves to participate in international associations. Of course we can translate some regional literatures into English and present them to the world; but this will be almost similar to the situation in which a man has the courage to sit in a gathering in borrowed clothes. The honour that one accrues from such a translation will be bestowed on an individual. And the world will not pay any attention to the language in which the book is written. The international recognition that literatures in French, Russian and Swedish have acquired is not due to their publications in English translation, but because they have been read and appreciated in their source language. Once they became famous, they started getting translated into English, German and French. If we want to acquire such a status in world literature, then we need to build a national language and on its basis we need to participate in the world literary congress. We can hope that at some point in time the one language spoken by 35 crores of Indians will get some publicity in the world but it is impossible that the twelve main Indian languages will acquire a status equal to the mature, major languages of the world.

In the concluding section of his write-up, while directing us to master the developed languages of the world, Nehruji has said,

Many amongst us should also try to master foreign languages. They would become our windows to see the world; they would usher in sunshine and fresh air. Many amongst us know English. We will take advantage of this, as it is a growing language; but knowing English alone is not enough; we have often been fooled as we only knew English. We have started seeing the entire world through the frames of English not realising that it is one-sided. Despite our political confrontation with the British regime, in many of our views and opinions we have become their slaves… if we read books and newspapers in French, German or Russian, then we come to know that there are other things in the world in which English has no significant role, as we have so far understood it.

But you do agree that it is difficult for a large number of our people to learn other European languages, and that is why you say:

> It would be pertinent to translate the well known books from foreign languages into Hindi. I find this absolutely necessary if we are to influence the perspectives and opinions of the world.

The books that we now translate from English get little publicity as most of those who would be interested in understanding them are well versed with English; and they would like to read such books in English rather than in Hindi translations; but such is not the case regarding translations from other European languages, as only a handful would know the source language.

We hope that our readers would reflect on this question; even those gentlemen who have this misconception that if Hindi becomes the national language then it would harm the regional languages, would now understand the existing nature of relation between Hindi and other regional languages. This would be the task of the Indian literary association and they would determine which books would be translated from regional languages into Hindi and how they would be placed in the forum of world literature. Though it would not be beneficial to regional languages if they are indifferent towards

Hindi considering it to be a separate language, it would of course harm the interest of a national literature.

[Editorial, *Hans*; November 1935]
Translated by Anuradha Ghosh

40. How can National Language be Enriched? (*Rashtrabhasha Kaise Samriddh Ho*)

We are happy to see that our leaders are getting more and more interested in the national language. In the week-long Hindi Prachar Saptaha (Campaign for Hindi), the speeches delivered by Janab Maulavi Jamal Ahmad, Shri C. Y. Chintamani[151] and other dignitaries emphasized upon the propagation and development of the national language, and all agreed on the significant role it had in generating cultural unity, but the President, Shri Rajendra Prasad,[152] viewed this question from an altogether different perspective. In his address to a public meeting in the South, he said that the national language can only be enriched through publicity and promotion. When it would be in use in the different regions and provinces, new words and phrases and new proverbs and sayings would get incorporated in it, and day by day, its repository would get enhanced. A part of the speech delivered is presented below:

> My point of view is that Hindi authors and readers should be requested to give up their horror of un-Hindi idioms and uses. The desire must be to absorb as many varieties of expression as are available to them. Some of the articles appearing in this (sic.) magazines, by their very nature, are untranslatable in Hindi except by a use of the local idioms. In such articles such idioms have been retained with a view to make the language more effective. Hindi readers must develop catholicity of taste and an anxiety to secure enrichment of expression by an absorption of expressive idioms of other provinces (sic.).

---

151. Shri C.Y. Chintamani (1880-1941) was a journalist and served as the editor of well-reputed newspapers such as the *Vizag Spectator* and *The Leader*.
152. Shri Rajendra Prasad was the first President of independent India, serving from 1952 to 1962.

Languages that are agile always enrich themselves by taking in words from other languages. Even now, we are witnessing how thousands of words and idioms from English have entered Hindi and are still flowing in, becoming a part of it. As English is a world language, it is developing at a very rapid pace. There is no such language in the world from which English has not borrowed to enhance its repository. If any English writer today wants to portray a scene from the Arab way of life, he would not be short of appropriate words. English has a relationship with countries like Mongolia and Brazil, Arabia as well as Africa, and in order to report and document news and stories, English writers need to use words and idioms from the languages there. In this way, the English language promotes itself and becomes wealthier by the day. Hindi has a wider reach than any other Indian language. But when it is becoming a national language, it has to take help from other regional languages. It is true, that care needs to be taken that in the passion for increasing its diction/vocabulary, it does not end up losing its essential structure and form. The Hindustani that is used in Hyderabad, is a corrupt form of the language, and we are forced to call it 'Dakhini' or 'Southern', instead of Hindustani. If Hindi too has a similar fate, then it would become 'Dakhini Hindi' or 'Southern Hindi'. It would be appropriate if we can enrich Hindi as much as possible by maintaining its essential structure and form. If the manner in which the non-Hindi speakers from Bombay and Pune, Mysore and Madras to Dhaka and Orissa, are using the language seep into the written form of it, then surely it would lead to the end of it. Just like English has a certain dignity and decorum that no one dares to transcend, though it is in use in different regions and nations of the world, Hindi too has a certain status that one needs to protect, no matter how much it spreads and widens its reach.

[Editorial, *Hans;* November 1935]

Translated by Anuradha Ghosh

41. The Boycott of Hindi and Gurmukhi in the Frontier Province (*Sarhadi Soobey mein Hindi and Gurmukhi ka Bahishkaar*)

Our Frontier government has presented a specimen of the kind of self-rule and provincial autonomy we are to acquire in the new governmental legislation. It is completely indifferent to the fact that the minorities have been granted some rights in the civilized world, and the protection of language, religion and culture hold integral positions therein; but what concern does it have with the civilized world? It has attained self-rule and it will develop a new policy, new legislation to publicly exhibit its tolerance towards the minority. Hence, why should it not also acquire dominion status? In my view, if the government is convinced of such relations between the minority and majority, it will very happily grant not dominion status, but complete self-rule.

The Education Minister of the Frontier Province is a Muslim gentleman. I have heard immense praise about his ethics and adroitness and he holds a high position amidst the well-wishers of the government. At least until now, precisely these qualities are the most important requisites to be a minister. Had the director of the education department been a European, the minister would have been free from all responsibilities. Who does not know that the poor minister is merely a puppet in the hands of others; dare he demonstrate his dynamism, he would have to leave the chair, and only very few are courageous enough to forgo their self-interest for the sake of their principles. Hence, had the director been an English gentleman we would have kept quiet, thinking that the minister was an object of pity. But when we see that the director of the education department these days is a Muslim gentleman, and the circular regarding the boycott of Hindi and Gurmukhi is his 'sacred' act, then not only that the minister cannot escape this responsibility, but the entire responsibility now falls on him. I can very well understand that an Indian minister cannot utter a word in front of a

European director, and if he did, he would have had it. But what I cannot understand is that how can an Indian minister remain silent in front of an Indian director? Against my will, I reach the conclusion that both the gentlemen are complicit in this boycott, but the responsibility lies on the shoulders of the minister because he is in this position just to protect the rights of the subjects, especially those of the minorities. The majority can protect itself, but here I see that those who are supposed to be the protector of the minority, is turning out to be its destroyer, and more woeful and shameful is the silence of those who should have fought against this policy on behalf of the minority. As far as I know, until now none of our Muslim leaders have raised their voice against this unjust, shameful, anti-national and narrow-minded policy. This could only mean that either the policy being enforced by the minister is being favoured, or it is not worthy of a verbal or written response from the perspective of justice. Such instances of impartiality and justice with which Muslims have ruled over others for centuries are found to be unparalleled in history. And today a person from this same community wrests the subjects of their due rights, and the leaders of the same community are sitting quietly.

And this spark has been released at a time when the gunpowder of bitterness, distrust and opposition is spread all over, with the fear of a nation-wide explosion. On the one hand there is an attempt to create a uniformity between Hindi and Urdu by erasing the differences between the two, and strike such an equivalence that it can become the national language of the country in a true sense. On the other hand, efforts are underway to further broaden this divide. Can we not appeal to our Muslim friends from other provinces to act according to the golden rule – 'behave with others only as you would expect them to behave with you'– and support the rights of the minorities of the Frontier Province on this occasion? In the roundtable conference, the Muslim minority had presented an absolutely legitimate demand, and it was also unanimously accepted, that the protection of their religion, language and culture could be ensured by the fundamental provisions of the legislation, so that they would have nothing to fear from the majority. Such provisions are the main pillars of every democratic legislature, which are universally accepted in the civilised world. But it is shocking that the same Muslim majority in the frontier province is attacking the cultural identity of the Hindu and Sikh minorities. We agree that mentalities keep altering, but not to such an extent that when they are in the minority, it is of one kind, and when they are in the majority, it is absolutely opposite. With its sectarian policy, has not the Muslim majority proven that there is a rationale for the Hindu Sabha's opposition to establish constitutional rule by all means. And when in this situation, one has been granted only limited rights and the majority is interfering to such an extent, what shall be the condition of the minority when the scope of the rights granted shall further widen? Two years ago the supporters of Hindi had made an absolutely legitimate demand before the Punjab government, that the ban on writing addresses on letters in Hindi be lifted and such letters may not be destroyed; it was so because a large section of the Hindus write letters in Hindi and this led to an uproar all around that Urdu is being erased, it is being uprooted, although the demand was safe and harmless in all respects. A few Hindi titles could not have obstructed the propagation and development of Urdu. If the entire country today starts writing addresses[153] in Urdu, then it would in no way greatly benefit Urdu and neither writing addresses in Hindi would enrich Hindi in any way. It was only the question of the sentiments of those Hindi-lovers who unfortunately could not read Urdu. That demand was rejected, although the number of Hindi-lovers in Punjab would not be less than 20 per cent; yet the people who opposed Hindi here would never tolerate that in South India, where the number of Muslims would not

153. Though *sirnaama* literally means 'title,' here it refers to 'address.'

be more than 10 per cent, the letters addressed in Urdu be torn and thrown away, and this should not be tolerated as well. Urdu is not a provincial language, and so is not Hindi, and neither of the two can be eradicated. Their development is collaborative, in spite of their differences. Both must get equal opportunities for their development, propagation and accomplishment. Are Urdu-lovers so thoughtless that they wish to divest others of the very rights they themselves are dying to achieve, and can they not imagine the distress, despair and regret they would have experienced in the same situation? This is exactly in tandem with the English tradition: what is considered nectar for England may be considered as poison for India.

We must deliberate upon the objective, which is to be accomplished through the initiation of this new policy. The Frontier Province wishes to educate its boys and girls in the language prevalent in the province, so that they can attain their legitimate place in the nation, and it is because of this that imparting education in different regional languages shall be ultimately disadvantageous. The common language of the Frontier Province is Urdu; hence the medium of education for everyone here should be Urdu, though English is dominant here anyway. If every province begins to follow this policy, there will be uproar in the nation. Although the Urdu-knowing population in most Indian provinces is negligible, yet there is enough provision to teach Urdu everywhere, and so it must be. Anywhere a group of six boys is willing to learn Urdu in Bihar, arrangements can be made to teach them. We believe that in some circumstances one has to take the support of such policies to merge the minority with the majority and to uproot all differences, one has to forcefully take refuge in such policy. But this is possible only in the situation when the minority does not have a language, literature or culture of its own. The Hindus of the Frontier Province cannot fall under this category. They have enough of everything that is required to grant them a distinct social status. Rather in certain matters they outpace the majority. Consider education itself. Out of the 31 middle schools in the entire province, 19 are being managed by Hindus and Sikhs. The number of Hindu girls is considerably more than Muslim girls. In the middle grade examination there were 6-7 Urdu-speaking girls compared to 169 Hindu and Sikh girls. The income tax paid by the Hindus to the government is also way more than the proportion of their population. In this situation any attempt to merge them with the majority is useless, just as it is, if the Hindu majority wishes to merge the Muslims in them, then that shall be their stupidity. Though I am not in favour of special rights, but keeping in mind the policy which the Frontier Province is following, the Hindus and Sikhs there should be given special rights.

After pondering upon all these conditions we reach the conclusion that whatever be the reasons that influenced this new policy, they lack the goodwill of national-interest. One could of course object to this policy from an economic perspective, but when the Hindi speaking population of the Frontier is a conspicuous part of the Province, its identity should not be set aflame on the grounds of an economic policy. No one can be deluded by the claim that this policy was well intentioned.

Our condition is worthy of such ridicule, shame and pity. We cannot make good use of even the few rights that we have got. At the same time, we, who are whimpering beneath the feet of others, do not desist in trampling those whom we can control, with our narrow-mindedness and lack of foresight. Until we free ourselves from this mentality and foster a spirit of goodwill for each other, whether we attain self-rule or paradise, we shall not get rid of this slavery. No matter how much the masters of our fate are happy to jump and prance around and beat their drums on our exploitation of each other, it still remains inadequate. One wishes that one could listen to the speeches on our activities that circulate in clubs with glasses raised in toast. Should we hope that the

Education Department of the Frontier Province will accept its mistake, which will be the biggest proof of their greatness, and will bury this policy deep within the bowels of the earth? My appeal to the Muslim leaders is to exercise their influence and broad-mindedness and desire for national-interest to save the nation from this catastrophe.

[Editorial, *Hans*; December 1935]
Translated by Mehak Sawhney

42. National Language of India (*Hindustan ki Qaumi Zabaan*)

On the above issue, Mr. Salim Jafar has written a bold piece in our Kanpur-based, fraternal journal *Zamaana*, which he concludes with the following words:

> If it is necessary to give birth to a new language, then Hindus and Mussalmans should agree that school-going children of both the communities be taught Hindi and Urdu simultaneously in schools, so that the importance accorded to the English language today is wrested from its roots by changing the language of communication in offices, making the law-courts use the language of the country to write their verdicts in and make the lawyers argue their case in it, as otherwise it would not be possible to curb the dominance of English.

Even today lakhs of Hindus read and write in Urdu, considering it their mother tongue. In the beginning, the Musalmans had taken Hindi to be their own tongue, but now, they consider it a sin to even look at Hindi alphabets. Would our Musalman friends agree to the proposal of making the status of Hindi compulsory till high school? We are convinced that the Hindus would not object to making Urdu compulsory till high school. If both these languages are made compulsory till high school then both of them would develop in such a fashion that day by day the two would come so close to each other that one day they would unite together to be one. If the Musalmans agree to this, then this would become the language of the country, in which all legal verdicts would be written and the lawyers too would argue in this tongue. Till the time the two languages are brought close together, English would continue to wield power and be in a position of dominance.

[Editorial, *Hans*; December 1935]
Translated by Anuradha Ghosh

43. Annual Festival of the Hindustani Academy (*Hindustani Academy ka Saalana Jalsa*)

The annual festival of the Hindustani Academy, Prayag, was decided to be held in the first week of January. On this occasion, the good writers and scholars of the provinces will come together, to speak on several topics related to literature and culture and read from their writing. For the chairmanship of the Urdu division, the Academy has invited the senior, experienced and dedicated Karmayogi,[154] Maulana Abdul Haque from the south. The President of the Hindi division would be the respected Dr. Ganganath Jha.[155] The gifted writer-cum-political analyst and speaker from Bihar, Shri Sachidanand Singh[156] has been elected as the President of the Festival. In this way, the Academy has introduced itself as inter-regional and inter-provincial in orientation. In our country, there are many provincial and regional literary institutions but till now there is no such institution that can invite creative writers from different regions and provinces to share and exchange their ideas. Hindustani is the common lingua franca of Bharatvarsha (India), and we humbly request the Academy to invite those in the service of literature from other regions and provinces as well on this occasion. This will not only make this Festival of the Academy more attractive but it will also develop Hindustani language and literature, increase the impact of the Hindustani language and extend our literary perspectives, enriching our repository of experiences. There are many questions pertaining to literature

154. 'Karmayogi' is the follower of "Karma marga" or the path of finding liberation through right action.

155. Dr. Ganganath Jha (1872-1941) was a scholar of Sanskrit.

156. Shri Sachidanand Singh (1871-1950) was a lawyer, parliamentarian, journalist.

on which we have so far reflected subjectively. The exchange of reflections in the deliberations will throw light on it and we will be able to rectify our mistakes and strengthen our views and opinions.

[Editorial, *Hans*; December 1935]
Translated by Anuradha Ghosh

44. The National Script (*Rashtra-Lipi*)

Important information about the national script committee is published in the papers from time to time ensuring that readers are always aware of the developments. In a previous issue of *Hans*, we published a piece by Shri Kaka Kalelkar on the same subject. In the December issue of *Madhuri*, Shri Venkatrao has published an important piece on the issue in which he has argued that minor changes in the Nagari script will not fully serve the purpose of a national script. An entire new script is necessary, one that could be learnt, written and printed in minimum time. In lieu of the Nagari script, he has invented a new script and also offered his responses to possible counter-arguments to the proposal of accepting a new script. Venkatrao's endeavour is undoubtedly worthy of praise. However, when we see that minor modifications to the Nagari script can bring it closer to the Bangla, Gujarati, Oriya, Gurmukhi and other scripts, and if we consider the literacy rate in these provinces to be even six or seven per cent of the population, it would still be tantamount to two crore people having to learn a new script. Since the origin of Tamil-Telugu is the Brahmi script, the closer we bring Nagari to the Brahmi script, the more proximate these Indian scripts become. There has been some publicity and propaganda on this issue, and hopefully the impracticalities in the previous efforts of the script improvement committee will disappear. Under these circumstances, we cannot support the invention of a new script. We need to take the whole nation along with us. The script improvement committee has formulated some new rules for conjoined letters in order to overcome the difficulties in printing, and I was delighted to know from Shri Hari G. Govil that he is developing a type whose components will be reduced from the existing five hundred to not more than a hundred and fifty. It will not only make printing easier and reduce publishing costs but also accommodate these new changes without any need for training. With a little practice, our eyes will become accustomed to this new form.

[Editorial, *Hans*; January 1936]
Translated by Rakesh Sengupta

45. A New Institution for Indian Litterateurs in London (*London mein Bharatiya Sahityakaron ki Ek Nayi Sanstha*)

I felt truly happy knowing that there has risen a desire even in our well educated and thoughtful youth to bring new vigour and awareness to literature. It is with this goal that the foundation for the Indian Progressive Writers Association has been laid, and seeing the manifesto that they have sent, there is hope that if this organisation continues, then literature will see the rise of a new age. Some parts of that manifesto is summed up below:

> There are momentous changes taking place in the Indian society. The roots of old ideas and beliefs are floundering and the birth of a new society is taking place. It is the duty of Indian litterateurs to portray the revolution that is taking place here and assist the nation in walking the path of development. After the destruction of the ancient civilization, Indian literature, distancing itself from the truths of life, has gone on to take shelter in worship and devotion. The consequence has been that it has become weak and sterile, in form as well as in substance. And, today, our literature is flooded with *bhakti* and *vairagya*.[157] There is display only of sentimentality; in a way, there has been proscription of thought and discretion. For the past two centuries, literature particularly only of this kind is being produced, and this is an embarrassing phase in our history. The aim of this association is to extract

157. *Vairagya* is a concept which connotes distance and detachment from those forces of life that are detrimental to the achievement of salvation.

literature and other arts from the dominance of the priests, the pundits, and the conservatives to bring them to a closer association with people, to rouse in them a sense of life and reality, by means of which we can brighten our future. While securing the traditions of Indian culture, we shall ruthlessly criticize the decadent instincts of our nation, and compile all these concerns through critical and creative writings, by means of which we can reach our goal. Our belief is that India's new literature should bring together the fundamental truths of our contemporary lives, and that includes our food, our impoverishment, our social decadence, the question of our political subjugation. It is only then that we will be able to understand these problems, only then will we gain operational strength. All that which takes us towards inactivity, torpor, and superstition, is despicable; all that which brings us towards a disposition of critique, that which encourages us to clamp the most beloved traditions also to the test of the intellect; that which makes us efficient; and gives us the strength to organise; this is what we consider progressive.

Keeping in mind these goals, this organisation has agreed to accept the following resolutions:

1) To create writers associations in the different linguistic provinces of India, and ensure coordination and cooperation among them through conducting conferences, distributing pamphlets, and so on and so forth; establishing close ties with provincial, central, as well as associations in London.
2) To maintain liaison with those literary institutions which, will not be against the aims of this organization.
3) Creation and translation of progressive literature, which must be flawless from an aesthetic point of view, by which we can banish cultural decay and can proceed towards independence and social upliftment in India.
4) To make efforts for the acceptance of Hindustani as the national language and Indo-Roman script as the national script.
5) Protection of the interests of litterateurs, helping those litterateurs who need help in publication of books.

6) Endeavouring for free thought and opinion.

The manifesto has the illustrious names of Shri Mulk Raj Anand,[158] Dr. K.S. Bhatt, Dr. J.C. Ghosh, Dr. S. Sinha, M.D. Taseer[159] and S.S. Zaheer[160] (sic.) and the address for correspondence is:

Dr. M.R. Anand
32, Russell Square,
London

We welcome this institution warmly and hope that it gains longevity. In reality we need literature exactly like this and we have set before us precisely this example. *Hans* has also been initiated for the same goals. Yes, we are not yet ready to accept the Indo-Roman as the national script, because we want to amend the Nagari script and make it so thorough, that it becomes equally useful for all the languages of India. I also want to say that if this institution can make arrangements for such literature which is compatible with its goals, to be translated into English and then published, it will be a real service to both—literature as well the nation. I want to request the members of the Hindi Lekhak Sangh (Hindi Writers' Association) that they give these proposals some thought and express their views. The goals of the Lekhak Sangh are also similar to the goals of this institution, and there is no reason why there should not be cooperation between the two.

[Editorial, *Hans;* January 1936]
Translated by Trisha Lalchandani

46. The Annual Conference of the Hindustani Academy (*Hindustani Academy Ka Varshik Sammelan*)

After four years, the Hindustani Academy, Allahabad, organised its annúal conference on 12th, 13th and 14th January

158. Shri Mulk Raj Anand (1905-2004) was an Indian writer of English.
159. Shri M.D. Taseer (1902-1950) was an Urdu poet.
160. Shri S.M. Zaheer (1899-1973) was an Urdu writer.

this year. Its President Shri Sachidanand Singh was a famous leader from Bihar, who was also a litterateur and a successful editor of *Hindustan Review*. It was a good conference of literary writers. They were divided into two sections—Urdu and Hindi. The head of the Urdu section was Maulana Abdul Haq Sahab and for the Hindi section, the head was Dr. Ganganath Jha. Highly scholarly and research-based articles were presented in both the sections, but due to both conferences being held simultaneously, the listeners did not get an opportunity to hear all the essays. If there was some arrangement for the invited guests to have stayed in one place together then there would have been opportunities to exchange thoughts and ideas and the value of this conference would have greatly increased. No, as evening came about, people left for their own accommodations and would return the next day at the stipulated time for the conference to begin.

Another loss of dividing Urdu and Hindi into two sections was that the wall that is emerging between the two, has heightened further. If both the communities cannot meet then they need not. If they want to beat their own *daflis* (a tambourine-like instrument) then keep playing on, but is there any harm if they at least listen to each other. If the number of selected essays would have been read jointly, then the feeling of them being separate would have reduced to some extent. Amongst all the essays, I found Maulana Abdul Haq's speech the most insightful. His speech had great force, enthusiasm and the power of great conviction. He rightly said that till now all the efforts for the progress of literature and language that have been or are being initiated have no consistency. Everyone does their own work in their own manner, no effort is made to benefit from the experiences and mistakes of others; the work that one does, the same is done by another, and so a lot of hard work and wealth go in vain.

The honourable President, while presenting a cursory overview of the various works initiated by the Academy, expressed the desire that such conferences should take place every year and scholars of other languages of India should also be invited. He shed light on the Hindi-Urdu dispute and requested both sisters to come closer and embrace each other. His words were as follows:

> While inviting Sir William Marris[161]to constitute the Hindustani Academy, Honourable Rai Rajeshwar Bali[162] said in his speech, that the Academy should attempt to promote such a language that can be understood by not only the educated but by all others as well. I have full sympathies with such a perspective. Sir William Marris said in his response to the Education Minister: every Hindi writer should have the objective that they are writing with Muslim readers in mind, and similarly Urdu writers should have this thought that they are writing with Hindu readers in mind.

In North India this issue is very significant for both literature and language and the President in his speech made an effort to solve this very problem; however the separatists did not find his attempt acceptable and after the conference was over, articles favouring separation are being written through letters and it is being proved that Urdu and Hindi have travelled away from each other traversing such different paths that for them to come closer is impossible and the attempt to make them come closer will lead to the destruction of both languages. Those favouring unity are being challenged again and again that they should compose such a piece that demonstrates in language the ideal of unity; it should not be a book of tales or stories; but it should be some historical, scientific, philosophical, or critical work. We ask our separatist brothers, with all due respect, that if there existed such a language then what was the need for such an organisation? The languages cited by Shri Sachidanand Singh in his speeches have led

161. Sir William Marris (1873-1945) was an administrator during the British rule in India and served as the Governor of the United Provinces between 1922 and 1928.
162. Rai Rajeshwar Bali (1889-1944) was the Taluqdar of Daryabad State, Minister in the State of Oudh (Uttar Pradesh).

to the revelation that the intentions of the founders of the Academy was not to create any new language, but to ensure the distinct advancement of both Urdu and Hindi and this organisation's name 'Hindustani Academy' was only chosen to be so because the 'Urdu-Hindi Academy' does not sound proper when heard or written. The hard work that our friend has put behind this discovery deserves compliments, but the emotions of Sir William Marris or Honourable Rai Rajeshwar Bali that were on their minds, on the subject of Hindustani Academy, do not seem problematic at all. They were not satisfied with the progress of both languages and it was for their improvement itself that the Academy was founded. To follow distinct paths Urdu and Hindi did not need any kind of governmental support; both languages were developing without its help.

But we ask, if Sir William Marris and Rai Rajeshwar Bali had founded the Academy for Urdu and Hindi to remain distinct, what is now our duty? Is it to increase or to reduce differences? If we have decided to increase it, then it is harmful for both literature and the nation. Our ideal should not be separatism, but unity. Having agreed on this, we would have to take a decision regarding our duty; and the most effective plan is to make both Urdu and Hindi compulsory subjects till the vernacular final and high school exams. Only then will the coming generation use the word that it understands to be suitable to express their ideas and emotions. And there are thousands of words like that, those which we can use even today, but the lust for language tricks does not allow us to use them. Dr. Tarachand's speech in Hindustani elicited raucous guffaws from friends, but I wish he was given an opportunity to speak at a public gathering where both Hindu-Musalmans of the illiterate or the less educated sections were present; then they would know that this was the language of the masses.

[Editorial, *Hans*; February 1936]

Translated by Soheb Niazi

47. The Hindustani Council in Delhi (*Dilli mein Hindustani Sabha*)

Perhaps it was for the first time in Hindustan that on 8th March, the Hindi and Urdu writers and literatti of Delhi's Jamia Millia together laid the foundation for a Hindustani Council (Sabha), which would aim to bring the literature of both languages together, generate love, compassion and unity among the scholars and litterateurs, give them a chance to understand each other's thoughts and ideas, and facilitate the growth of Hindustani. There was a time when, despite the lack of progress of knowledge and talent, and lack of awareness in politics, there was great love among people. In the field of literature too, there was no distinction. But times took such a turn that Hindi became the language of the Hindus and Urdu that of the Muslims. Hindus started to turn their faces away from Urdu and Muslims from Hindi. Two distinct camps emerged, and both languages and their literatures got caught in the web of politics. Ill feelings began to grow amongst them. Any attempts to propagate Hindi started being seen with suspicion in the Urdu circle, and the propagation of Urdu in the Hindi circle. Though literature has no relation to politics, its subject is 'man' and no matter what label he puts on himself, man remains man. However, this is the age of politics, and there is no enterprise which can remain untainted by political narrowness. The result of this practice is that Hindi votaries are inept in Urdu and Urdu votaries know nothing of Hindi. Whatever is written in Urdu is done bearing the Urdu readers in mind; whatever is written in Hindi is done keeping Hindi readers in mind. Why should the Hindi writer consider that there might be Urdu readers for his writing, when that is not the case. The Urdu writer has no such freedom, since there still remain some people from the older generation who love Hindi and Urdu equally, because they consider the two as forms of the same language. Yet these people are so few in number that they cannot be considered significant in the progress of literature and language. In this manner, both languages are moving further away from each other, and how will we grow close to those with whom we cannot converse freely in our own language.

Unfortunately, Hindi and Urdu literature passed through an era when literature had broken all ties with ordinary life, and all their efforts were invested in writing about sorrows, lamenting about the pain of separation. At the most, people would write in praise of liquor or lament and philosophise about the world's transience; but the literatures that are close to life are the ones that have written the history of the nation and inscribed its culture. A writer of literature is the torch-bearer of a nation. His heart is filled with the light of love. There is no room for intolerance and narrow-mindedness. These writers are the ones fighting against war today. Is there any such revolution whose seeds have not been sown by writers of literature? It is undeniable that the unification of a nation comes through its cultural unification—an objective that can be achieved only through mutual friendships, exchange of thoughts and kindness. There is no other means to achieve the unification of language other than this. Spoken language takes birth in streets and marketplaces, but the language of literature and culture will be born only in the society of scholars. When a writer of Urdu reads his composition before an audience that also includes Hindi writers, he will attempt to write in a language that is intelligible to Hindiwalas as well. Similarly, a Hindi writer will be compelled to make his language intelligible to the Urdu circle. And if this plan too, like others, doesn't slacken, then in the days to come we can hope that just as both Hindi and Urdu were born in Delhi, similarly the Hindustani language and style will also develop only in Delhi. The biggest hurdle that the propagators of Hindustani have come across so far is that they are inept to write an informative piece in the language. If the Hindustani Sabha (Hindustani Council) makes provisions to start even a small magazine in Hindustani, it would be a great service to the nation; it will also be extremely encouraging for those who are supporters of Hindustani, but don't use it for the fear of being mocked at, since they are very few in number. We request the secretaries of the Sabha (Council) that they notify about their meetings in newspapers, so that people may get informed about their achievements.

[Editorial, *Hans*; April 1936]
Translated by Sarah Mariam

48. The Reality of the Indian Literary Council (*Bhartiya Sahitya Parishad ki Asl Haqeeqat*)

Giving a brief account of the meeting of the Indian Literary Council in the pamphlet 'Urdu' published from Hyderabad, Maulana Abdul Haq Sahab has written such things which in my opinion are borne of some misconceptions, and in the light of such misunderstanding, I am afraid that the Council might have to wash its hands off the support given by the Urdu segment. It, therefore, seems necessary to present my thoughts in an effort to erase those doubts. When the Indian Literary Council invited the representatives of all literatures of India, it was done so that all of us, abandoning our political differences, could partake of this literary enterprise and experience oneness at least in the field of literature. If the agenda of the spokespersons of the Council was to only campaign for Hindi, then it needn't have given invitation to all other literatures. The campaign for Hindi is being carried out through the Hindi Sahitya Sammelan and the Nagari Pracharini Sabha; why would there be a separate body for this work? There was one and only one goal before us, that there be such an organisation in Hindustan where litterateurs of all languages meet one another, ponder over the new, perplexing questions that plague literature and society, critique the new trends in literature, and in this way, there will arise the feeling of being part of a strong fraternity among them, there will arise a feeling of confidence, they will get to know other literatures, and they will find inspiration to fulfill the lack that they see in their literature. Everyone believes that if Hindustan is to be kept alive, it can stay alive only as a nation; only as a nation can it secure its position in the tradition of the world and retrieve its lost pride. As discrete nation states, its condition would then be the same as it was during the arrival of the Muslims and the British. None of us desire that our regional biases take such a shape again which makes one region see the condition of the other in the clutches of the enemy from an idle distance with a hateful glee. I feel no apprehension in proclaiming that there was no sense of nationalistic feeling before the arrival of the British. It is true that the sense of nationalism here was not as strong or well-developed as it is today, though such a feeling was already underway in Europe. It had not only risen, it had even taken full shape. India's unorganised, scattered public had to succumb to the organised nationalism of the British. There is no doubt that even then cultural unity in Hindustan was present to a certain extent, however it was of the kind which is found in the nation-states of Europe. Everyone believed in the *Vedas* and the scriptures, just as the whole of Europe believes in the *Bible* today. Everyone was a devotee of Ram, Krishna, and Shiva, just as all of Europe is a devotee of Christ and other great saints. Everyone took pleasure in Kalidas, Valmiki, Bhavbhuti, and others, just as all of Europe takes pleasure in Homer, Virgil, Plato, or Aristotle. Despite that, there was no national unity among them. This unity is a gift of the British; though the British rule has brought about immense damage, it has also done some good to us, and that is an awakening of the sense of nationalism. Now it is our duty that we take advantage of the situation and make this feeling so alive, so intense that it is not shaken by any threat. The disease of regionalism is once again gathering strength. Its signs are clearly visible. We are already beginning to forget the lesson we learnt in the two centuries of slavery, even though the same form of slavery continues to persist even now. It is my conjecture that with provincial autonomy, regionalism is going to grow stronger, enmity between provinces will increase, and the feeling of nationalism will weaken.

Besides the goal of a literary organisation, campaigning for the uncontested literary ideals, and literary support, the Bhartiya Parishad also envisioned the goal of bolstering our sense of nationalism through organisational support. It was never our intention to hinder the growth and development of regional literatures through this endeavour. If our mother tongues are distinct, our literatures will be different too. If, despite being discrete provinces, we could exist as one, we would not have any need of such an endeavour; albeit we believe that our future lies in the hands of national unity. Our life and death depend on it. And, unity between language and literature exists in many aspects of national unity. Hence, in the frame of literary unity, the question of one language also arises unsolicitedly, much like an uninvited guest. The question of script also follows the question of language. And, these questions raised their heads in the Council's meeting too.

The dispute was over language—to be precise, over the form of which the Sahitya Parishad should assume patronage. The word 'Hindi' vexes Urdu just as much 'Urdu' vexes Hindi. The bias is not simply in the name. The manner in which Hindi is being written, it is rid with Sanskrit words. The manner in which Urdu is written, it is rid with Arabic and Persian words. The intermediate version of both the languages is Hindustani, which claims to be the language of the vernacular, wherein words from no language are sacrificed, if they are commonly used. Hindustani may not be a favourite of Hindi, however Urdu has not had any hiccups in accepting Hindustani, for it appears to be its very own. However, the Council, instead of adopting Hindustani as its medium has adopted 'Hindi Hindustani.' The Urduwalas could not comprehend what 'Hindi Hindustani' meant, perhaps they thought that it was merely another name for Hindi. They misapprehended that conjoining Hindi and Hindustani was being unjust to Urdu. It is being mired in this suspicion that such words escaped Maulana Abdul Haq's pen:

"There was a time when Mahatma Gandhi had written a letter in his own hand to Hakeem Azam Khan in Hindustani, that is, in the Urdu language using the Persian letters, and today, let alone Urdu, he does not even like to write or hear Hindustani. In his correspondence, he has mentioned not once but numerous times that if only 'Hindustani' was used in the resolution, it would be read as Urdu; however, this thought did not occur to him while using the word 'Hindustani' alone in the resolution of the National Congress. What is the exact reason behind it? What could be the factors that have led him to adopt this strange and shocking revolutionary stance? After pondering over it, one understands that the cause for all this alienation and change, machinations and strategies, is the unfortunate politics of our country. Until the time Mahatma Gandhi and his associates were hopeful that there might be some political bargain with the Muslims, they kept repeating 'Hindustani', which was an effective lullaby to put everyone to rest; however when they lost hope, or when they found such a bargain futile, they flung their guise away and revealed their true selves. They may campaign for Hindi as much as they desire. If they cannot abandon Hindi, we cannot abandon Urdu either. If they throw their weight around thinking that they are well-equipped and influential, then we too are not underlings."

I feel pained seeing these words from the pen of an experienced, thoughtful, senior man of principles such as Maulana Abdul Haq. The Council in which he sat had a majority of the Hindiwalas. There weren't more than three representatives of Urdu. Despite that, when there was a vote between 'Hindi Hindustani' and 'Hindustani', there were only a little less than half of them who voted in favour of 'Hindustani.' If my memory serves me right, there was a division of fifteen and twenty-five. Having fifteen votes in favour of 'Hindustani' in a gathering which is Hindi-centric and which has three supporters of Urdu is a victory despite the defeat. It is highly possible that in a second gathering, the support for Hindustani would have grown stronger. And it is not surprising that more supporters of the Hindustani which hasn't come into use yet have not revealed themselves. Even those who have assumed authority over Hindustani—and it includes the writer of these lines too—have not been able to give any new shape to Hindustani yet. They have only managed to conceptualise it, which means that it should be a language that is in the form of a confluence of both Urdu and Hindi, is facile, and belongs to common parlance. It is our responsibility as supporters of Hindustani that we campaign for it, that we give it such shape that those in favour of Urdu as well as those in favour of Hindi embrace it. Hindustani Councils have been set up in Delhi and Lahore. They may be set up in other cities too. It should be their duty that they make an effort towards the progress and propagation of Hindustani; and that which is merely in the imagination at present may transform into reality. I request Maulana Sahab to not have such great hopes from the Council prematurely, and to not suspect intentions. It is possible that which seems unmanageable at present may become achievable in a year or two. With the presence of merely three people in favour of Urdu, the consequence was that the Council conceded to incorporate an amendment on language in their resolution. He must not jeopardise the fate of the Council by giving in to hopelessness from now on.

[Editorial, *Hans*; June 1936]
Translated by Trisha Lalchandani